IN THE LIGHT OF DAY

STEVE LAMPI

WESTBOW
P R E S S®
A DIVISION OF THOMAS NELSON
& ZONDERVAN

WestBow Press books may be ordered through booksellers or by contacting:

WestBow Press
A Division of Thomas Nelson & Zondervan
1663 Liberty Drive
Bloomington, IN 47403
www.westbowpress.com
1 (866) 928-1240

ISBN: 978-1-5127-3911-4 (sc)
ISBN: 978-1-5127-3912-1 (hc)
ISBN: 978-1-5127-3910-7 (e)

Library of Congress Control Number: 2016906406

Print information available on the last page.

WestBow Press rev. date: 04/26/2016

CONTENTS

CHAPTER 1—THE BEGINNING

THERE WAS A ROAD THAT GENTLY SLOPED OFF OF Main Street in Brighton, Michigan. This street was lined with houses spread out about twenty yards from one another. The lawns were green and usually cut uniformly. Mature maple and oak trees grew around the property lines and provided shade for the neighbors' backyards. Coming off the sloping street was a small red house on the left with the number 221. Hanging above the garage door was a basketball hoop that began what would literally be the one-shining-moment basketball career of yours truly. I hit a three pointer in a high school game while being fouled by what seemed to be a seven-foot-tall giant. At 5'9, everyone seems like a giant on the basketball court. Yes, the crowd went nuts, and yes, I still reminisce about that shot. When you only went in for the last two minutes of a game up by 20, that's what you hold on to. Benchwarmers represent!

In the backyard of this house was a fenced-in pool that relieved the heat of summer days for the many neighborhood kids. If you were to walk in the front door of the house, the stairs would be to your left leading to the bedrooms. Mine was the one to the right, down the hall, straight ahead. In the evenings you could hear the distant sounds of the passing trains alerting the intersection of their oncoming presence. Over the tops of the trees, the sound of the train would make its way to my ears. I can't remember a night without the faint whistle humming through the city and the rumbling of the tracks following along. The window of my youth faced the woods. From this window hung a ladder that could be used as a fire escape, if one should happen. I used it to imagine myself as a fireman— that was until my mom told me to stop climbing up the side of our house all the time. I was a boy, so if it could be climbed, I would give it a shot. To me, this room, this place is home. Not because I live there now, but it's where I was a child. It's where I could appreciate a calm morning or the colors of a sunset without any plans, deadlines, preparations, text messages, phone calls or any other demands that come with everyday life. Lately those sunsets have gone by without much thought.

My Name is Stephen. I go by Steve. I often get called "Stef-en," and I've had many conversations as to how the last e makes the first e say its name, at least in my case. As a child I can vividly remember my father giving me bull rides on his back. I want to say he took it easy on me, but I remember feeling terrified at his great strength as I held on for dear life, never really breaking that eight-second mark to score. My mom was always kind to me and rarely raised her voice. Every year she asked what kind of birthday cake I would like. Somehow it always turned out to be a spaceship. Either I really liked spaceships or my mom had no desire to make a He-Man, Thunder Cat, Smurf, or Tecmo Bowl cake.

She did her best I'm sure. That leaves my brother. His name is Jeff. For those of you with siblings, it probably doesn't take much to know how our relationship was growing up. We fought, laughed, hurt each other, drove my mom and dad crazy at times, and then did it all over again for 18 years until he went to college. He then became my best friend.

Now as a grown man with a family of my own, I live in a city that boasts one of the largest chemical companies in the world. If it's true what they say about the colors of sunsets being related to air particulates, then I should be seeing some of the best sunsets on earth, but I don't notice a real difference. Not that I've been comparing, but it seems a Lake Tahoe sunset has nothing more than the same effect on the sky as a sunset in the vast expanse of fields we have here in Bullock Creek, Michigan. I believe it's not only the light of the sky that makes a great sunset but also what's hidden within the passing light. In the end, the beauty we see in the daylight takes on a different portrait when the light begins to fade; it is still beautiful, but somewhat hidden. What the light reveals in the day takes on a new view through the passing light. There's something hidden within it, and it's a shadow of its true self, making it hard to see as it is tucked away in the darkness.

I have a maple tree in my yard that comes to life every spring. The lush green leaves hide its winter barrenness as the warmth of spring arrives, giving way to rain and the health it needs to flourish. It's a lot older than I am—thirty-six years old. I've noticed its growth the last three years since moving into our house. It's doing so well that my neighbor has suggested I trim it back a bit, to which I replied, "Yes, I should trim it." It is not trimmed yet. From afar, it looks healthy. Little would you know it has a disease or some kind of imperfection where the leaves take on dark spots. The closer you get to the tree, the more you notice its imperfections. Something is not functioning correctly within the life it has. We can identify that there is a problem, but we are limited in our ability to help it. When the sun begins to go down, the tree once again looks healthy, but I know it's not perfect. Someone who has never taken the time to look would never notice it had the issue in the first place. They could walk by the tree for years and miss it if they never stopped to see. The sunsets make this even harder to recognize. Those spots are still there, but they hide so well in the evening.

Think about our relationships. We know our family differently than we know most of our friends. We know how they react in certain situations. We know what makes them happy and what ticks them off. We can produce one of those two emotions in them because we know them so well. My wife has the uncanny ability to make me feel as if I could conquer the world while revealing my weaknesses with just one look. Yet even with knowing our family, we typically have a "sunset knowledge" of most people's true selves. We don't see as much of them as we do our family members. We are limited in knowing their thoughts, feelings, and hearts. We spend time with them, but compared to our family, we know them only within the sunsets where the imperfections are hidden, much like the tree in my yard.

The same can be said for humanity at large. We are beautiful as a creation. Not only do we find attraction in a person's beauty because of what they may look like, more importantly, we find story after story of humanity's capability to reveal the picture of love, dedication, sacrifice and care. I have a friend who overheard a conversation between a woman and another man about her troubles trying to pay for a family member's kidney dialysis that he was in desperate need of. My friend got ahold of her contact information and called to tell her that he wanted to help. Before even asking how much the treatment would cost, he had already taken out a sum of money that he decided to give her—whether more than or less than what she needed. As the woman listened to him on the phone, she wept. They met up at the local Radio Shack, and he handed her the gift. She had no words as she stumbled over what to say. Humanity—that's what I'm trying to portray when I speak of our beauty. There's someone in need, and another willing to help.

Society has been trying to fool us about our humanity for years now regarding beauty, as if beauty could be limited to the outward appearance of a man or woman. As if beauty's worth could only be determined by those with perfect skin and desirable features. If that's the case, then the beauty we have desired is all but fleeting and wasting away, and we've traded what defines beauty in humanity for mere attractiveness. A person's beauty can be whittled down to a fraction of who they really are by concentrating our attention on what is outwardly seen. We have believed in many cases that our primary concern for acceptance is found in making what is seen "attractive" or seem "successful" while minimizing the needs of the heart.

Not to be outdone by our society, my high school hosted an annual male beauty contest every year. The so-called "hottest" guys from every grade would partake in a male version of the Miss America Pageant. Shirts off, answering questions that were way too deep for the event's atmosphere and strutting around like arrogant meatheads as girls screamed. I was there in the stands as an overzealous mocker. It was mostly a chance to make fun of friends who made the mistake of being a part of the competition. Some participants were naturals, while others were deer in headlights with really defined abs—all for the glory of being "hot". In the end, a winner was proclaimed, and for a moment he enjoyed his reign until the next year when someone else won and he was long forgotten.

I am not hot. Seriously, try to do a workout program with three young children. More power to you if you've pulled that off, but I am way too tired at the end of the day to workout. Running in the backyard with kids, mowing, cleaning out gutters and organizing my garage works all the core areas. I'm good. I hope what people would understand of me is that there is something about me that human eyes could never see. Deep down I bet most people would feel the same way, no matter what they may look like. We are of worth, not to be treated as something someone else can meet their own needs through but truly of great importance, despite our past. Because in the end, when darkness comes, we are all capable of hiding what we really look like, just as the maple tree does in the evening.

When the sun is setting and the dark creeps in, what's revealed is only a shadow of who we really are. We are not fully known by others within this fleeting light, and many people find themselves living in the sunsets. We hope the oncoming night and passing light will reveal a bit of our beauty but hide what is perceived unacceptable or, in many cases, too real. Our "spots", our imperfections, have driven our entirety into hiding. It's a humanity problem. We hide. We've always hidden. We've found solace in the darkness, but our worth is not lost, and our value has not faded away. We are fully known, even in the darkest of nights.

This is going to be about you and me. Just as my friend helped the woman with her family member's dialysis, there is something no one on this earth can deny. We all need help, and I am talking about something much deeper than counseling or therapy. It involves a place no person could ever reach. The depths of the human heart are too unfathomable for humanity to search out in one another. We need a light capable of revealing what is hidden in the sunset. We need to once again look out the window to listen and watch. Like a child, we must not be too overwhelmed with the many distractions, pursuits, and troubles of life that we forget to slow down to see something beyond what consumes our thoughts. This may allow our eyes to take in what is true and real, not only in regards to others, but more importantly, our own hearts. We must be aware there are things in this world that will take great advantage of our soul and heart through lies and empty promises. There have been moments we walked into and trusted those promises but have come out hurt. There have been moments where we have hurt others. It is a part of our existence and the moment we live in.

We must recognize the sunset again and be aware of the portrait it paints. As we acknowledge its beauty, let's not forget it's revealing only a glimpse of the worlds true self. We cannot forget that daylight is on its way—another sunrise breaking the dawn, revealing the hearts of humanity. What we may not see of another's heart has been seen. An ever-present light is upon us. Creation longs to be seen and known, demanding the light of day.

You've chosen to read this book. I don't know exactly how you came about it, but somehow you opened it and began reading. You've decided to take time out of your life and possibly listen to what is being said. You need to know, that as you read on, I am for you and hope you would understand help is here; that you might see there is a purpose in the revealing of the tree's spots. It's needed. It's necessary. These "spots" are an unavoidable part of everyone's life. The life we live now is vulnerable to darkness, but there is no need to hide for acceptance. We all have our spots, we all have hurt, but what remains hidden from humanity will not find shelter from the light. When someone is close enough to see the struggle within and provides a way out, it's our opportunity to take hold of what we need and begin to trust.

Remember as you read this: the one writing these words has been through the brokenness and has also caused it within this world. I am in no way claiming perfection to anything I may write about. I am human, and I struggle. I'm learning and have learned that the human heart is longing, mine included. It's in need, and through many conversations with men and women, young and old, two truths continue to stand out: We all need help, and we all long to entrust our hearts to something or someone. This search leads us in many directions and into numerous circumstances. You've opened this book, and I don't believe it's a coincidence. As you read on, I invite you to hear more about this light as we discuss its beauty in the pages to come. In the end, there is a help and trust that lasts, and light guides the way.

CHAPTER 2—THE KNOWN

IF MARRIAGE IS AN ADVENTURE, DATING MUST BE A vacation. Vacations are for getting away from the constants in life or a welcomed change of pace in life. Adventures are for facing the unknown and the challenges that may come about as you go. I have had many conversations with men who have been married a lot longer than myself, and one resounding theme you hear from most husbands, no matter the age, is they are still trying to figure out their wives. Yes, they know their wives. Of all the relationship these men have, their wives are the closest to them, but two obstacles remain within all people, whether single, dating, or married: We are human, and we are limited.

I was in the first year of a new job and was getting my feet wet in understanding how to balance what I did for a living, marriage, and fatherhood. Late one night, I arrived home to my wife in tears. She sat on the stairs with my son in her arms, and all she had to say to me was, "I hate your job." I had it coming, and I knew it. She let me know that she needed more from me as a partner in marriage. She needed me to be there for her and our son. She felt alone in this adventure of raising a child. Her tears and words revealed much of the necessity of her heart that I was unaware of at the moment. This helped me understand her need because I knew I had been missing out on what is more important than putting hours in at work. I love my wife. I do my best to be a good father and husband, but I can say that I have missed the mark of perfect love. I've had that same conversation more than once since that initial encounter on the staircase. I am only human, I am limited, and in my imperfection, I love imperfectly. For all of us, we may not mean to love imperfectly, but we can't escape it.

If I were given a dollar every time I felt as though I could have handled a situation differently with my wife, children, or friends in the past ten years, I might be able to retire. I'd be in Colorado while listening to the waters flow across the rocks in a nearby river. I am rich in my limitations as a husband, father, and friend at moments. I am absolutely incapable of being everything all of them need. I cannot do it. This is no excuse to be a lazy or ungrateful person, but you and I can't fulfill what the human heart longs for entirely: to be fully known, every need, and fully loved.

This is where the truth about each of us begins. Every person reading this book will have this in common: one hundred percent of the people you know do not fully know you. They don't know the weight of the pain you've been through, the shame you've walked in at times in life, the fear you may have, the way you may have mistreated others, the ways you have been mistreated, the struggle that consumes your mind for periods of time, or the feelings of joy that are inexpressible within your heart. They don't know the things you've thought about, the desires you've had, the depth of anger that has led to hate, or the forgiveness you've battled in giving to another. This does not include the numerous instances and experiences that remain silent within us. We live fully unknown when it comes to the depth of our hearts. We will even live in darkness, hiding the things we have done or have gone through, so that we would not miss out on being accepted or loved. We have held back what others could never see or know about us, and even if we told them, they are still limited in making things right again. This is our reality. We can't get around it on our own, and we find solace in knowing we are yet loved with an imperfect love from others. For everyone, this is our sunset, and these are our spots.

My wife has access to my heart, but I can't explain to her the depths of what I feel at times. The same can be said for her. I know her heart and longings to a point, but I cannot fully understand them as they are within her. I know some of her past hurts that are a part of her life story. These hurts may be the reason she lives a certain way now, but by no means does that translate into me understanding her feelings wholly. Her mom passed away four years ago, and it was hard for all of us as family. In the end, I do not have the memories or the relationship my wife had with her mother. I am limited in knowing her, and I cannot cause the sorrow she has to dissipate from her heart. I do not fully comprehend the pain she experienced; I've not walked there yet. If only I could, I would be able to understand her heart a little more than I do now, but I do my best to listen. Most of the time, that's all she wants.

Facebook has given many people with access to the Internet the opportunity to meet the need of being known. The tag line is "Facebook helps you connect and share with the people in your life." But let's be honest, it should read, "Facebook, where your longing to know someone is listening to you is fulfilled."

Snapchat, Vine, Youtube, Facebook, Twitter, and Instagram have become a necessity to many hearts in being known. They satisfy the longing we have to be "liked", "seen", or "followed". They give us an opportunity to express our thoughts on other people's thoughts. They have given value to our words when they are "shared" and fulfillment for a moment when what we post merits a response. Whether the feedback is positive or negative, at least someone has heard us; we count. Someone recognized we are here and gave us a sense of value. That's why when we post things, no matter the avenue, no one is immune to the feeling of "please acknowledge me." It may be subtle within our thoughts, but it's there. Our society has found an easy fix at the tips of our fingers that can be used whenever we want, without having to hide or feel shame, and without having to admit any type of issue because everyone else is doing it. It has no impact on our physical health, but it often leads our hearts to what will fade; only to draw us back to satisfy the feeling of needing to be acknowledged. It has met our society's greatest desires: to be known, valued, and heard. And in it, we don't have to truly reveal anything more than what we want to reveal. There is great need met within the heart found in social media, but there is an even greater danger in depending on the feeling of acknowledgement it can give us.

For the most part, these social media outlets reveal sunset words and pictures, hidden behind a screen and only what one wants to portray. There's nothing wrong with desiring to be heard, seen, to connect, or encourage through these avenues. Once again, it's in us to be known and to have worth in others eyes, but the need met through them is only a handful of sand in the vast beach that is our heart. And our hearts are in search of the peace found in being accepted and loved.

In 2002, I was twenty-two years old, and I found myself in a large white van with three other friends picking up passengers in Panama City, Florida to provide safe transportation around town. While doing this, we invited everyone who rode with us to a pancake breakfast the next morning. While fulfilling this good deed, our van became too full to pick up any more passengers. Jason, (the driver and now brother-in-law) who has a kind and willing heart to help those in need, decided to implement that heart and fit a few more in the van that was already at maximum inebriated people capacity. I wondered, "Where are these people going to sit?" Those entering the van solved that problem on their own. Two scantily clad girls found themselves a spot on my lap. At that instant, I went into full shutdown mode and held my breath. It was the longest five minutes of my life, mainly from the lack of oxygen. Troubled with the entire situation, I looked out the windows and acted like what was happening was normal. The girls seemed totally fine, unaware of my presence. Needless to say, I did not get their names or invite them to the pancake breakfast we were offering the next morning as I was asked to do. In the moment, I wasn't concerned about their names, but what I am aware of now is they actually had names. They had stories. They had a purpose in going to Panama City for spring break. Maybe it was to party or to have fun. Maybe it was to find someone else they had something in common with or to hook up with another person. One thing I can't speak of, though, is the depth of those girls' hearts. I will never know what was going on, or has gone on within them, to drive their desires to be there. It's not my call or my great concern to understand that. The only thing I had to offer was a van ride to their next destination, or a moment to share in the beauty of humanity by helping them get there safely.

As the person helping others down in Panama City, one would think I am the one to be praised, but that's not how humanity works. As I was there I walked, talked, ate, and helped others as someone longing for help and to be known. What nobody knew of me was I had my own issues I kept within, hidden in the sunset. I didn't trust anyone or believe anyone would understand the weight of the shame or sorrow I was experiencing. While everyone I went with seemed to be celebrating a lot and getting much out of the trip, I was in regret for life's past choices; hoping I could mask them by doing something out of the ordinary.

Growing up, I watched my mother go through the pain of having two brothers commit suicide. At the time, I had no idea why they took their lives, but I did know they struggled with substance abuse. This stayed with me throughout my high school years, and when I went to college, I had trouble disassociating drunkenness and destructiveness. I believed people who drank too much had a very good chance of hurting or killing themselves. This was my mindset; this is what I experienced. Sadly, I saw first hand how I could be right.

One night during my freshman year in college, I was waiting for my roommates to come home from partying when one of the girls I knew came back to the dorms, clearly intoxicated, with another guy I had never seen before. She stumbled into her room and the stranger followed. I followed them both into the room as well. I didn't trust him. She was absolutely gone, vulnerable in her drunkenness. He looked at me while she lay on her bed, passed out, and asked if I was going to leave the room. I said, "No." I sat there in silence, hoping it would become uncomfortable enough for him to leave. I can remember him feeding me a line similar to, "You can leave. I will take care of her." I told him I would just stay and wait for her roommates to get home. After some time, he got up out of the chair where he was sitting and stumbled out of the room. I took a deep breath in relief. I had never been in a fight before, but I was ready and he was drunk—I figured I had good chance. I left and closed the door behind me. The rest of the evening, I waited for a group of my friends to come home. The next morning I sat with the same girl at breakfast, frustrated and mad. She had no clue what had happened the night before, so I told her the whole story. I didn't know how she would react, but I cared for her, so I was honest. She did begin to see the seriousness of the decisions she was making, becoming much more cautious after that, and over time we became good friends.

That night, as I waited in her room for the stranger to leave, was one of the best moments in our friendship. It wasn't about me. This friendship grew into my first dating relationship, but I was unsure of how to navigate those waters. The problem was I wanted her to be someone she wasn't at the time, and in doing so, the simplicity of friendship we began with was damaged by the expectations of dating. I stayed for the feelings but was ignorant to the reality of what I was doing. This could only last for so long, and in time, what I believed would be everything I needed was gone. I left that relationship knowing I could have treated someone that I cared for much better than I had, leaving guilt and regret within my heart.

That's where I could relate with many people in Panama City. I was searching and thought the pattern of life, and what it led me to, would be enough to satisfy my heart. I was caught up in chasing after what made me feel better temporarily. I believed a relationship would sustain the depth of longing in my heart for acceptance, worth, and love. Whether the relationship was long term, short term or only a few days, it would not have measured up to the depth of what I truly needed. Like I said, this is where I could relate to many people in Panama City. Sure, maybe I was aware of the longing to be known more than others in the large white van, but my lack of trust in those around me drew me to a place of hiding to be accepted. The "sunset living" was able to distort the real image of what was going on within me. What seemed content was hidden in distrust.

If the light of day revealed what was really going on, those I went down to Florida with would have seen a clearer glimpse of me as an individual. That, to me, was not an option, and I'm sure the girls I met in the van have had those moments in life too; where acceptance was more appealing than revealing the reality of the heart. It's why humanity will hide. We are often afraid that someone will see our spots, and realize we are imperfect, or in many cases, in need of help.

Hiding is an inescapable part of our being without light, but why and what are we so afraid of? We celebrate relationships magnificently. Weddings, engagements, and reunions are a time to celebrate how we've committed to love and friendship. Yet, in each of these areas, there are limits set internally by everyone involved. Some of those limits will never be reached by anyone but for good reason. It is not a place another person should tread vainly, trying to completely accomplish what humanity could never fulfill in someone else's heart. Expecting another person to understand and carry our heart is not something we should presume is possible. We can lighten the burden or sorrow of life through the friendship we have with one another, but these relationships could never fully overcome what so deeply affects our lives. It may seem we've been close to others, but not close enough. Love from others helps in the healing; it's our beauty, but the remnants of guilt, hurt, pain, or sorrow will still linger.

The gift of conversation keeps the heart known in a relationship. To reveal what is going on within our feelings, our thoughts, and our struggles are where mankind finds friendship and commitment finds longevity. When we dialogue, we are opening ourselves to the opportunity to help and the opportunity to receive help. This is how we were made to function: communicating our need and communicating our love. When we hide, we ignore both of these needs. Hiding leads to many people becoming distant, depressed, angry, unforgiving, bitter, slanderous, and sadly at times, hateful. The sunsets are not as pretty as we thought for our hearts. In moments they seemed beautiful and peaceful, but where the past resides cannot be overcome by a conversation or an encouraging word unless light reveals what must be seen and known in the presence of what can truly help.

Have you ever had the feeling you cannot possibly help someone more than you have already tried? It's like you dove as deep as you could into someone else's life or have allowed someone to glimpse the depth of your own heart, but either way, we were not capable of reaching those depths. It's as if the heart is an ocean, and the deeper someone dives, they soon find themselves crushed under the weight of the water's pressure and bail out. Family and friends listen, but for many things, and in many ways, are left helpless. They cannot go any further on their own power to understand your thoughts or feelings. The spots are seen, but there is nothing that can be done within their capability to make everything right again. They help, but won't be capable of a reaching where the heart finds it's deepest longing and need. The help of others is only a CAT scan when we need an MRI to reveal more of the problem, leading to a lasting answer.

This is where the truth matters. This is where light matters. This is where the heart finds its rest in being fully known and fully revealed in light. It's where our purpose meets contentment and struggles no longer with what humanity can't accomplish for anyone else on earth. It's going to be okay. We desire appreciation from others, but we don't need to thrive off of it in truth. Yes, we long for acceptance, but we don't need to run to others or numerous activities, companies, or organizations to remind ourselves of our great importance. Yes, we desire to be known and loved, but we live in a world that has been saturated in darkness, which strips the capabilities of humanity to satisfy fully. This is where the beauty of humankind finds the limit it cannot breech but gives way to the light that has made us fully known and in being known, fully loved. Whether you have found yourself as a helper or a passenger in the Panama City van, we need, and somewhere within, long for this light to shine on us—that it would reach where no one else can. It is necessary for humanity to understand they are known. The light reveals and shows us things we need to see and be aware of. Our spots are fully seen; coming with a promise of healing that can only be answered through light itself. This light shines into the darkness of what lies within us, and no one can truly live without it.

CHAPTER 3—THE BEAUTY AND THE BROKENNESS

I HAD GOOD FRIENDS IN HIGH SCHOOL. I DID NOT hang out with a lot of them apart from school or sports, but they were good friends to me. As a junior and senior in high school, one of my closest friends was a boy named Mason. I called him Mase. Mason was, what I would say, fearless and funny. Hilarious would be an understatement as I think about him at the age of 17. He made everyone laugh in numerous ways.

I remember our car rides together; it seemed like we drove everywhere, including track practice. He was a pole-vaulter on the team. Sometimes I would drive him to practice, and we would destroy the speakers in my 86' Mercury Tracer. No, that Mercury did not attract the eyes of car enthusiasts, but it could play Stevie Ray Vaughn's Best Hits loudly. I recall him putting the song "Little Wing" on repeat while thoroughly enjoying Stevie's face melting solo as he played the air guitar. I tried to teach him to play guitar once, but he didn't really take to it. One thing that made Mason stand out was his passion for professional entertainment wrestling. So much so, that he and his friends started the BWA (Backyard Wrestling Association) in our hometown. On any given evening you could find Mason and other participants throwing one another off of cars onto burning chairs or from houses onto tables to the cheers of a few, or of many, depending on the event location. Being around him made many people smile, laugh, and at times shake their heads because of his fearlessness.

On December 28th, 2008, Mason was faithfully fulfilling his commitment as a police officer; it was late at night. He pulled a teenager over during a traffic stop, but the boy had no ID. Mason drove him to, what he was led to believe, a residence where a responsible adult was living to confirm the identification of the young man. Soon after the door was opened at the residence, the boy began to scuffle with Mason and eventually got a hold of his gun. He then shot and killed Mason, taking the life of a father, son, brother, and friend, while punching his own ticket to a lifetime behind bars. A devastating event that changed many lives in a single moment.

I was sitting next to the fireplace in my basement when I read the news of his death. All of a sudden I was 17 again, but this time the laughter and joy turned to sorrow and heartache. I wish with all my heart I stayed closer than I did with Mason after high school, but no matter our relationship at the moment, my mind began to unload the memory bank of our time together as kids. I did the only thing a boy does when he doesn't know what to do. I called my mom, and I remember telling her frantically that Mason had been killed. She didn't understand me at all and had me slow down.

When I finally pulled it together, she understood and wept with me. She knew Mason because he spent time at our house, but I think she cried mostly over my sorrow. She felt my hurt at the time and knew my heart was broken.

The beauty of friendship we have with those closest to us will eventually, whether in a situation as this or for some other reason, experience brokenness. It can be from tragedy, arguments, a fall out, or even death. Brokenness cannot be tamed in our world. It cannot be bridled and told when or where to go. It cannot be overcome by man's will, and time may relieve the pain but will not quench its anguish fully. It will happen amidst the beauty of what we experience in this life without warning, and many times, without explanation.

Beauty and brokenness: they co-exist. A glimpse of what is right, and the sting of what is wrong within the world. These moments hurt and reveal the result of our wrongdoing. This is why light exists; it shows us the difference between the two. We can discern what is right at times, but we all know within humanity is darkness. We may have not committed the most terrible of crimes, but we have caused hurt to others. This again points to our inability to fully love one another with spotless compassion, unfailing grace, unwavering mercy, and pure selflessness.

We've seen glimpses of this love, but even as we celebrate the love we see, humanity remains broken and limited. With that comes a very sad outcome: broken people will inevitably break others. Whether we know it or not, we have hurt people. That is why humanity itself will never be the answer for mankind. A boyfriend, girlfriend, wife, or husband will not fully complete us. The moments of beauty we see and experience with those we love most will not fully overcome the brokenness of what has happened to our lives or what we have done to ourselves. There is a very real place within the heart of mankind that can only be occupied by truth. All other people and things, given the chance to reside within the heart, will eventually fail in their attempt to completely set things right again. It is a beautiful thing to watch people walk with and carry each other through hard times in this life. I have carried and have been carried, but the truth is we have a need that runs deeper than what any person can satisfy.

I love organizations that help people. There is a company called Tom's Shoes, and for every pair of shoes bought, Tom's gives a pair to a child that is in need of shoes around the world; often times saving their lives. So simple, yet so needed. Gap's Red Campaign has been fighting for babies being born with HIV in Africa by donating funds from certain clothes to provide needed medicines that can help the cause. United Way is a community organization that focuses solely on awareness of needs within a community and meeting those needs. Beautiful things can happen through broken and imperfect people. But the reality is our world will never fully give the needy and hurting what will satisfy completely. Whether it's poverty, hunger, medicinal needs, or clothing, we do not have what this world is longing for. We meet the temporary. We alleviate the pain within the brokenness, but by no means can we fully solve the real problem within our world. Keep fighting, humanity! It's good to keep fighting, but understand we are limited.

We see only glimpses of the true light that overcomes the darkness of those around us here. Our home—this world we live in for a moment, is not right. It is hurting and it is longing for more. This desire is for something lasting, not fading, something that will heal fully and not simply alleviate for a time being. Amidst the beauty of life, brokenness awaits around the corner.

The reason for this, once again, is you and me. It's people. It's our lack of capabilities to comprehend and carry out how to make it all better. It's our inability to fully know how to fully love because we don't fully know the heart of others. We know we are limited by the years of our lives, and we are. We all know in our death the world will still hurt. There has not been one man walking this earth that could fully come through on his promise to make a social situation reside forever. Martin Luther King Jr. gave us awareness and pushed for change, but look, we are still having the same struggles. We've seen change and what he did was right, but humanity will prevail in its attacks. We are not the only country that struggles through racism. It is a global problem because people live all around the globe. This world will only continue on in brokenness as long as humanity is at the center of our hope. It's as if we need someone to save us from ourselves, and we've all contributed in some way to the pain of this place. We've wronged others, and we've hurt others. We, too, have been hurt and would be foolish to deny that we desire a perfect love and a world with no more sorrow, pain, tears, hurt, wrongdoing, brokenness, and suffering—a world where we are all content.

Contentment is one of those words that often gets a bad wrap for its lack of feeling. No one wants to simply be content in a relationship or situation. You don't hear many people saying, "I am content with him/her." That makes us sound like we have settled for something less than what we really want. The contentment of being in the light is synonymous with joy. Joy is not synonymous with happiness. Joy speaks of a hope beyond what we are going through, and happiness is reliant on how we feel within the moment. No one can claim to always be happy with everything in life, but when light reveals our hearts and the help we need, we find the contentment of a joy that lasts. A joy that can slow down this pursuit of fleeting happiness and put our feet on something permanent. This is what our hearts truly desire—a joy that lasts.

Look around. Can't you see it? The world at large is longing for something other than what is fading within it. Everyone, in some way, desires this world to become a better place, whatever that may look like to each individual. Out of this longing, man has created thousands of ways to hope for something more, thousands of pursuits that will only satisfy temporarily, and thousands of promises that cannot save us from the brokenness of this place. We are fathers and mothers; we are friends and family, grandparents and loved ones. We have great gifts in this life and so much to be grateful for. Yet the human heart still has an unexplained gaping hole in which hope, beyond the beauty of what we can be seen, can only satisfy. We long for more. It's the girls in the van in Panama City longing for more to satisfy their need of love and acceptance, or a feeling that they are being noticed. It's why we see some of the most "beautiful" and wealthy people in this world destroy their lives in the pursuit of perceived happiness.

Now we begin to see the light. Now we begin to see a glimpse of the reality; our brokenness opens the door to the light of the world. In our longing and our pain, we begin to understand the purpose of suffering. The light shines in the suffering, in the sorrow, in the pain and hurt, the wrongdoing, and in the brokenness. It rejoices in the creation of humanity as a father watching a child being born and has given us a glimpse of itself by allowing us to suffer. In suffering, we long for something better—something lasting and eternal—what our hearts cannot help but hope in. A new home, a new place, where beauty is without brokenness and death cannot possibly be the final outcome of true life. We brought the brokenness on ourselves, yet the light overcame it. We loved the sunset, but there is only one true never-setting light. He alone can heal and bring us home. You were made to live in this light where darkness is no longer our hiding place, only a testimony to the overcoming power of the light within our lives.

At just the right time, light was revealed. The light of day—the light of humanity—became known. And in this light alone is that longing met. The longing for men and women everywhere to be fully known, even as we have hidden in darkness, has been met with an unfailing, lasting love, and a hope beyond the empty pursuits and promises we've given our hearts to.

CHAPTER 4—THE INTRODUCTION

THINK ABOUT SOMEONE YOU HAVE A CLOSE meaningful relationship with. There are probably certain traits within the relationship that must exist for it to be legit and of substance, such as trust, love, and respect. These attributes are universally important for a true friendship. One of the major defining factors in a meaningful relationship is consistency. No matter how far apart one has been from another, no matter the distance or time, when we see that person again it's as if we saw them yesterday. There is no getting reacquainted because you know they haven't changed in your absence. You know their heart and who they are, even as years pass. They are consistent.

This is where we find our desire to stay and our longing to hold onto those relationships we find worth in. They have great value. We pay money and travel thousands of miles to go and reconnect with those we have a true friendship with. We make sure we don't miss the opportunity to be together, to laugh, and to simply be ourselves in their presence. No fronts need to be put up because there is no fear in what our friends may think of us. We can relax in those relationships because we trust them and know they are familiar with our hearts more than most. Even in the things our friends know about us, they still love us. When we are with them, it's part of the beauty of this world.

Imagine holding a relationship down based on trying to payback a person through good deeds, money, or following some strict guidelines. Imagine going to spend time with a friend out of obligation or guilt rather than truly wanting to be with them. Some find that consistency in a relationship is based on how they act or what they do for the one they are with. The moment they falter in fulfilling the expectations of the other person, they begin to worry about what could happen. The repercussions can produce fear. Will they be left? Will they be accused or condemned? Will they be hurt? Will they have to come up with more excuses as to why they messed up? This is not love nor is it of worth to the human heart. It's empty and shallow, yet people live this way. At times, it can be in ignorance or desperation for affection. This has never been the reason for light. Light does not reveal the need or inability of our hearts to love perfectly only to leave us in fear as we search for justification of our short falls. Within this light is love, and love does not demand proof of our worth. It pursues us beyond our measure of deeds, and whether we've lived up to our side of the relationship or not, it is foundational in understanding the purpose and reason for this light within our darkness.

Religion is often met with duty. "Am I doing?" Following the rules or doing what is "good enough", in our own opinion, has enslaved humanity to its own definition of good. We are now allowed to judge our own lives by the way we define the extent of what we believe "good" looks like. So the question is this: Whom are we comparing our goodness to? Compared to someone who has committed murder we look like angels, our halos glowing bright around our big fat heads of how "good" we are. Compared to Mother Teresa, we look lazy and half-hearted in our effort to be a "good" person. Who says we are good? Based on what? What are we testing this belief against? Is it a general look of life? Do you follow more closely the traditions or requirements of your faith, feelings, morals, or values? What if someone has followed them better than you? Is it someone who volunteers their time over 3 hours a week? I don't know how to determine goodness. I help with after school programs, but does that make me good? I know it is good to do those things, but in the deepest part of my being, does that make me good? It doesn't seem measurable. So the only thing left for mankind to do is to test our character based on others' character to reveal our goodness. This is where we begin to have the thought, "I don't do that, so I must be a good person." Of course, we find others we feel are not as good as us to test our own character against. Take a glance at comments on the Internet or Twitter. It makes many people feel better to slander and speak out against the darkness in others rather than admit or be shown their own.

But no one is left without sunsets. We have spots that are unseen by others, and we hide to remain unseen. We fear what others may say about us if they find out, so we look for a comfortable corner in the sunset to live in. But no one can truly hide forever. That's where many have heard or used the phrase, "God knows our hearts." I agree, and to be honest, this is where our problem begins.

Let me be clear: doing good things for others in this world is right, but we are in no way capable of measuring our own personal goodness without light. In the light is where our wrongdoings and spots are fully seen. The full picture is revealed. We do not have the understanding of the human hearts around us to speak against someone's wrong and stay silent about our own. We cannot see the past hurts or struggles within a person that shows itself through the decisions they've made. The problem is that we have followed our own evil desires into darkness, but have not had anything to test it against except man's definition of what is good and acceptable. Our issue is not that we love doing good or being a part of something that is important to us. Our issue is that when tested against true light, we are not good. Everything is seen; everything is known. We are not right when the light of day begins to shine on us. Our spots are discovered. Just as the maple leaves have revealed their true selves in the sunlight outside my window, our imperfections are revealed. We begin to understand that we have a problem, and that problem is called sin.

Here is where a relationship is formed through true and lasting love, paving the way to life. None of the deeds we have done will take away the darkness of our doings. I am going to be honest with you: remember when I said it's as if we need someone to save us from ourselves? The light of day is the light of the world. He has come to do just that—to save. You may know his name or be familiar with his role in history. You might be familiar with his ways, but nothing will matter more in your life than truly knowing him, and living in his light. He is intimately acquainted with our hearts. In fact, he was there in the beginning of you. Even before the first breath you took as a baby on this earth, he knew you and gave that coming breath to you. He formed your being and took delight in you more than any friend or loved one ever will.

You are the created one. He was there in the beginning and will be all that's left for humanity in the end. He is hoped in with an everlasting joy by millions upon millions of people throughout the history of this world. He is healing for the broken and has given eternal worth to all humanity. He is not far off from any of us, and in this truth and light, the human heart and soul has been seen, known, and loved. Our hearts will not remain hidden because of him, and our soul can alone be saved through him. His name is Jesus.

Jesus means "God saves" which defines his purpose. Humanity needs true saving, and we cannot hope in ourselves to accomplish that. He is the light that reveals our hearts darkness and our inabilities to be good enough before an absolute perfect God so that we would clearly see our need for his grace. This grace is one that cannot be earned, but only given by and through him. He knows our hurts and pains. Many of these hurts, we've brought upon ourselves. We have not only hurt others, we have the capability to hurt ourselves because of our inability to see the light of life that leads to truth, and truth saves. In the rejection and ignorance of this light, we find darkness. This leads to pain and hurt, no matter how intense or tolerable that pain may seem at the time. He offers life beyond what is seen and visible in the sunsets of our lives on this earth. His words teach us to live in that light and how to love others because of his love for us, yet never promising perfection in this moment we live. There will be suffering in this world, but it's in the beauty of his light, overcoming the brokenness, that mankind now has something to hold onto that will last.

Two thousand years ago, this man Jesus faced a lost world within its ideas of truth. His proclamations of who he was took him in front of a government that beat him with whips. They broke his back open to bleed. They placed a crown of thorns on his head, mocking his authority over the world. Then they made him carry a wooden cross to a hill where they nailed his hands and feet into it as he agonized in the death of crucifixion. This is historical and this is real. He is not a fairy tale nor simply a good teacher or tradition to celebrate on December 25th. He is God, our Creator. He then breathed his last words within that time period. Within those words he spoke, "Father, forgive them, for they do not know what they are doing." We did not know what we were capable of doing as we did it. Even today, in the darkness of sin, we are unaware of what we are capable of doing to our lives and others. As Jesus hung and died on that cross, he died because of His Father's love for mankind, overcoming the sin that was so prevalent and destructive to those he loved. Jesus fulfilled his promise in overcoming this sin that previously left us imperfect, spotted, and blemished within, causing separation from God the Father and his loved ones, you and me. Then Jesus, the light of the world, breathed his last breath and it was finished. The light now overcame darkness, and humanity had a way back to the Father. God's intolerance of our blindness to truth and inability to save our own selves, was shown as his son hung on the cross. This is eternal love; it is not found in Hollywood movies or written by our favorite authors. It's given by God alone, covered in the blood of his son. The love God had for this world sent his son to the cross. And in humanity's belief and trust in Jesus as a needed Savior, it is now possible to live with God eternally.

When I was seven-years-old, I decided to walk home from a friend's house with my eyes closed to see if I could make it to my yard by memory. I've walked home from his house, which was right across the street, hundreds of times. It was so routine I didn't even have to think about it: down the hill, curve a tiny bit to the right, then walk straight. So, with confidence in my ability to accomplish this feat, I took a deep breath, closed my eyes, and began walking. I still remember: I felt the rocks of my friend's unpaved driveway shifting and moving beneath my feet. Then came the soft touch of the grass between my toes. "Surely I am almost to the road," I thought to myself. I began to cross the street with a sense of pride and accomplishment, for I was almost there. The road was paved and warmed by the sun. Tiny stones resting on it pushed against the skin of my feet, but I pressed on. I was close; I knew I was about to reach my yard. Bam! I ran my face into our mailbox. Immediately I went into the fetal position because I thought I lost my eyeball. I opened my eyes to a double vision I could not shake. I cried because I thought for the rest of my life I would be seeing two of everything. My mom was there to bring me inside. I told her what had happened, and I'm sure she restrained herself from laughing at my vain efforts.

Our confidence in our ability to live this life apart from truth—no matter how bold or courageous we are—will reveal our limitations. It may seem we know how to walk without the light guiding us, but darkness will get the best of us eventually. We will feel the brokenness in some form. No matter how much we believe, "We've got this", we will eventually come to the end. We will reach the end of ourselves and the mailbox is not moving for us. We will clearly see we are in need of someone to save us from sin and ourselves, unless we once again try to temper it by turning to something else to subdue the reality of our need. This is where we find the light, opening our eyes to life and truth. The truth helping us understand love, grace, mercy, discipline, right, wrong, and the growing desire to love God in a relationship rather than in our religious traditions or pattern of life that has shown itself fleeting. We can stop relying on our own power and knowledge to walk home with our eyes closed. Yet the Savior sympathizes with our weakness, and he understands our struggles. Whether past hurts, present circumstances, or any pain to come in the future, he can relate. Jesus was one of us. He was fully human while here, yet never faltered in the darkness. How? He was the light. Untainted by darkness, perfect and pure, nothing could darken his way as he depended on and trusted in the Father God.

This Jesus lived among us. He walked this world. He was the beauty of love yet received the punishment of sin.

The shadows and sin of humanity that have followed us throughout history needed to be revealed so they could be destroyed in the light of God's Son. He is that light we all need. He saw how the darkness deceived and blinded people to the light of truth and life. His offer to humanity was one that had to happen for life to be once again full, forever, complete, and restored to the Creator—our Father.

What we could not do, he did. Our life and purpose is to have an eternal, lasting relationship with a perfect Father and God that created us. Jesus came to make that possible. He lived, loved and told others of God's plan to save this world from its sin and brokenness. God sent his son, Jesus, to save the world and to reconcile what was broken back to himself because he loved us. His Son, Jesus—this man who the history of the world is written around and came to existence through—lived perfectly and died perfect on our behalf. He suffered and went through pain to take the punishment for our imperfection of sin and wrongdoing against God. There had to be sacrifice in love for forgiveness to heal, and Jesus' death is God the Father saying, "You are forgiven." This event took place on a cross. It is a large wooden structure meant for torture and pain. It is meant for a slow agonizing death because of one's wrongdoings. Here is true love that lasts. In his perfectly pure light, without any wrong committed in his life, Jesus died a sinless, perfect man; taking the punishment of sin away from humanity by dying the death darkness and sin leads to. Death—that is our outcome as we hope and live apart from a faith and trust in Jesus Christ. Sin leads us to death, destruction, and darkness, but in and because of

Jesus, one finds the sting of these conquered by life in his salvation.

This was not only to save, as he does from death, but to restore humanity's relationship with God, our true Father. He is pure light and cannot fellowship with darkness. That is why the Savior was sent. And the Savior loves us as the Father loves us, for they are one. The Creator knows you better than you know yourself. He knows our hearts most and desires you to know his. This is amazing! God the Father sent God the Son, the light of the world, to save us. It was their desire because they love, and this love cannot be stopped. God knew and saw us in our brokenness and delighted in our worth. In our sunset darkness he saw the need for light. But because of our sin, the darkness we have walked and hidden in, we could not know him fully until the light of day—Jesus— made his way into this world: In doing so, he gave humanity hope and life through his death. He revealed the darkness of our hearts and illuminated the shadows to make us right and good, so we may experience fellowship with a perfect God. The spots of guilt and sin that marked our lives would become spotless and leave us forgiven in the eyes of God. All this done by him and for him because he first desired us before we desired him. Darkness cannot have a relationship with light. They are in conflict with one another. It's like water and fire. They do not exist together; one will overcome the other eventually. They fight to overcome, but one will eventually prove too strong for the other to remain in existence.

We have seen the images of the destruction that fire has caused in people's lives. Families lose homes and loved ones in these terrible events. They walk through the rubble, trying to find anything left untouched by flames. We see firefighters walk out with children in arm becoming renowned rescuers as they hand the child to a parent, saving something of indescribable worth. You have worth and are of the greatest worth in the eyes of God. Jesus, His Son, was sent and walked into overwhelming destruction, coming to rescue those from sin and death. The destruction we have walked in and watch others walk into has not yet overwhelmed us to the point of death. He has carried us out of the sorrow, grief, pain, or heartache guiding us into the safety of the hands of our Father. He alone can rescue and overcome in this way.

Jesus has overcome what would have left humanity hopeless within the darkness. The light has and will overcome for all who look to him and reach out for help. What we could not do, He did. Jesus made us right in the Father's eyes through his death, paving the way to an everlasting love beyond the darkness of the grave. God longs for our hearts to call him Father, so he gave his Son. He desires us to love and know him, so he sent the one he loved and knew to make that possible. He desires a relationship with men and women everywhere that are still hiding in the sunset or bound in the darkness.

When I was twenty-three-years-old, I worked at a camp for cognitively and physically impaired children; I had no idea what I signed up for. All I knew was I loved working with kids, so when my friend asked me to join the team, I gladly applied for the position of a camp leader. There was a staff of about 10 college-aged students; we were goofy kids that had a heart to help others. It was an amazing opportunity, but it had its moments of difficulty. I learned a lot about myself through working at the camp, mostly through a young child named Charlie.

Charlie was cognitively and physically disabled. He was 8-years-old and blind. Every morning I would wake Charlie up at 5:00 a.m. because he would wet through his diaper and all over himself. Charlie was unable to wash himself in the shower because of his disabilities, which left the job to me. After walking to the laundry room to wash his bed sheets and clothes, I would give him a shower. All I could remember is that he loved the water. He would splash around in the shower as I tried to bath him. He would laugh, and I would have to tell him to quiet down so he didn't wake up the other kids in the cabin. That never worked. As he was having great fun, I was absolutely exhausted. Each morning, for the duration of the camp, I fought to keep my eyes open. My thoughts went to his mother and how tired she must have been. She deserved a break, even if it was only for a couple weeks.

Where Charlie was incapable of cleaning and caring for himself at that time, someone had to step in. Someone needed to do what he could not do on his own and help him in a way he could not help himself. But after that camp was over, I missed Charlie the most. He was worth every second, every laundry run, every early morning, as well as every time I had to help feed him during meals. I had no one else to help in those endeavors; he was my responsibility, and he was worth it. There was a glimpse of light for Charlie in those weeks. Someone cared, someone helped, and there was someone who loved him. I learned a lot about love in those weeks with Charlie, mostly the sacrifice that comes with it.

The literal darkness Charlie walked in daily due to his condition is much like humanities inward condition. We have trouble discerning how to overcome darkness or brokenness and must be guided by light to experience a love that truly outlasts what we have done or gone through. Someone had to step in to accomplish that on our behalf. Here is the light, the light of life that guides all mankind into truth. And as the light reveals truth, the truth sets us free to truly live, laugh, and have joy, even in our struggles. Charlie laughed a lot, even with his limitations. This life is meant to be lived in joy and hope amidst the unknown within our world. Whether it has been losing a loved one, a broken friendship, a battle with disease, financial struggles and stress, an abusive relationship, being mistreated, an absent parent, or doubts of one's importance, everyone has tasted the failing promise of the world's gains, and we cannot stop it from failing. But Jesus leads us into truth, saving us from those false assurances while placing our hearts and minds on the trust found in a very meaningful and necessary relationship to life.

Here is love that lasts for the human soul, the sacrifice worth seeing. The longings for something lasting have been met in the everlasting God. He was going to redeem what humanity could not make happen. We could only find ourselves walking through the rubble in search of something that lasted, but nothing in this world made it through the destruction of sin. Our hearts attempt to say, "I can do this alone!" or "I don't need you!" to the giver of life has left us wanting and wandering in the night, hoping to find what endures. Everything within this earth has now become temporary and fading apart from the everlasting God.

The beauty we see is only a glimpse of what is to come. The love we know within the relationships we have is a taste of the love many have to look forward to within the Father's presence. This is the one true lasting relationship offered to mankind for eternity, and in him, many will live together forever. He desires you and has shown love to this world by sending us light, and in that light, for those who come to Christ, he calls us children and desires nothing less than that type of relationship with us—one of worth and value, one that lasts beyond death, not one that is promoted through obligations or pursuing of what fades, but one that is experienced through true, genuine, and everlasting love. Those who have acknowledged a need for him find true love. They find great joy in knowing there is nothing they need to prove of their worth to him. God desires us to know a love that surpasses what we know of love apart from him, so I'd like to introduce Jesus—God loves you.

CHAPTER 5—THE UNCHANGEABLE ONE

THE SKY WAS ON FIRE A COUPLE OF NIGHTS AGO as I sat by a bonfire with a group of students and some friends. We all noticed it. The sunset was unique, not just another sunset. The light looked different. Every night, there are pictures painted in the sky all over the world. They look and take different shapes, forms, and colors. Each sunset is unique, yet made by the same sun every day from the beginning to the end. No other thing can take credit for its breathtaking views and peaceful moments it creates in the craziness of life. To take the time to look and see these sunsets, while ignoring the world for a bit, can remind us of the beauty that has been made or provoke the calmest of moments we all need—leaving us in awe.

Oddly enough, when we are with others and we are looking at these sun-made portraits, rarely do you hear a word. Maybe there is a small conversation about what they look like, but we mostly stand quietly and watch. Something we cannot touch, something so far beyond our reach, has shown itself to us, but we cannot control its coming and going. It will fade into darkness, and we will be left with the billions of stars of night as we wait for our one to awake us the next morning.

Inevitably, our star will rise again and will guide us into our sleep the following day. We are at its mercy, and we have based our rising on its presence. If the sun were to not faithfully show itself, we would be left alone in the dark. All creation would suffer together its absence. It would confuse, cause unrest, and create havoc because we depend so deeply on its consistency. We rely on its faithfulness to never change its course on us.

The same cannot be said for the promises of humanity. We will always change course. Things wills shift. We have heard of change and have seen change amidst our societies and within our families. Beliefs and ideas change within the world, leading us into different times. These shifts have and will always be constant. Some rejoice amidst the change and some become discouraged. Humanity changes for the good that progress can bring people, but at the same time, change can lead us toward the destructive things of the heart. We have incredible ways to connect with people on the Internet and incredible ways to hurt people through it, as well. This is just one example; it can help and it can hurt. The changes of man will find ways to reveal beauty and brokenness within the shifting beliefs and convictions amidst our pursuit of what we think will benefit humanity. We can see this happen in the political realm of our country that creates so much dissension at times. It's birthed out of a desire to be right, hoping we can control the process of making our country or world better. This may not be the case for all, but there is undeniable tension present in our society because of our desire to change. We believe certain changes are right and will lead us in an appropriate direction. But as we know and have seen, that direction doesn't always lead where we thought it would take us, so every four or eight years we hope in change.

All of us can be thankful for change. Without it, we could still have people suffering from Tuberculosis and Polio in our country or find the difficulty of reaching out to troops across the world to send them our love. Certain technological advances have provided a way to accomplish amazing feats. The Civil Rights Movement was a needed eye-opening change for America. Change can be good, but we are so fortunate to have an unchanging light whose faithfulness surpasses that of anyone, or anything, this ever-changing world could know.

Jesus was and is the light to the world. This light was proclaimed in unchanging truths, so as to not leave the world in the dark. If what he proclaimed were capable of being changed, it would prove itself as a lie or only a momentary movement of passion, but he remains an unchangeable light and truth. This is to be greatly appreciated but is sadly misunderstood. The light revealed what needed to be seen about the depravity of our sin. It can be hard for us to hear but necessary to save us from sin's destructive grip. There is a common theme that runs through all humanity: we are often lost in a world that changes so frequently as we follow along, unaware of the real outcome. At what point will progress and change be enough for our world? Our continual longing to make this world right, in our opinion, speaks of our hearts desire to create something that someday will satisfy fully. Sadly, we fight and stand up for things that will always be changeable. At what point do we stop trusting in mankind movements to make our lives full? As good as they can be, they will melt away into the inevitable search for something else, change. The light is faithful every morning, just as Jesus is faithful at every moment of our lives. We don't need to follow along in search of what the world promises will make our lives better. This is where an unchangeable truth saves us from a desire to hope in humanity.

In many cases, this truth has been taken and twisted to our own pleasing, which has led to the inconsistency of empty self-pleasing pursuits that only leave us in the night. Addictions, affairs, drugs, fame, and the love of money have been leaving people empty for centuries because they can only unveil momentary happiness. This, in the end, leaves us in darkness—chasing our tails of what we believe will provide what is lacking within our hearts. God has and always will, in his truth, frustrate and overcome that darkness we have hidden in or live in. His desire in truth is not to fight with humanity but to reveal. After all, he has no need to fight. He alone has the authority to speak what is infinitely unchangeable. So, what is said within his Word will last into eternity, not changeable by any man, any woman, any movement or any higher court. Why? Because he loves, and his desire is for us to live in his light and not try to discern what is real and true within darkness. It's too hard to see in the dark.

The truths of Jesus that he taught us were spoken in love. Love is not always a pleasing word we hear. It can cut and can convict. It can demand change within a life. But we have taken the light of truth and have believed it is changeable and there to be interpreted as we please, not as it is. Even amidst that belief, the light of truth still does not change. Truth can never change. Man's proclaimed truth will find failings, but not so with an all-knowing and loving God. And if the light of Jesus Christ is unchangeable, then that alone leaves us as the ones who need to change. But if we do not desire to change within his truth, then our next best bet is to change the truth to fit our own longings. This is where we find ourselves in the dark. We excuse ourselves from God's truth and begin to live our own ways—apart from what is true, absent of light, and hidden in sunsets. We are leaves in the fading light littered with sin, guilt, and spots because we lived apart from the light of life, Jesus.

Fall on college campuses should be fun. My home state of Michigan has amazing autumns. The leaves change color and the air becomes crisp. Students wear their hoodies and light jackets. Saturdays are reserved for friends and football. We enjoy the morning over a cup of coffee or a long walk. The leaves draw us out of our houses into nature, as if the trees are telling us to "come and see" what's happening. I see the changes every year, yet it is still amazing even though I have lived here my whole life. The same can be said for what we believe in. Every morning something draws us out of bed that says come and see. This is found everywhere. The "come and see" could be this promise of what a degree may get you, so off to 8:00 a.m. classes as a student. The "come and see" could be a friendship you enjoy, so off to breakfast or the coffee shop. The "come and see" could be a job that pays the bills, so there you find yourself again, whether enjoying the job or tolerating it.

I went to college because I saw what it promised: a better life, fun, friendships, and a great experience. The "come and see" aspects of college for many are basically the same; they just take a different form and look. Some students go to college to succeed and are driven by studies. Some people go to find the balance of studies and the experience, and some others go to throw caution to the wind because the "come and see" was mostly a promise of freedom and unadulterated bliss for oneself.

My senior year in college, I came, I saw, and I did not conquer. The promise of what I assumed was worth my time and what I thought was going to be so beautifully fulfilling, found its end—just as the leaves that change color do every year. I ended up a branch: much worse, a branch covered in ice from the winter freeze. The promise that carried me to college had run its course. The "come and see" that seemed to be so amazing for the last three years had finally fallen off of the tree. My counselor looked at me and said, "Just graduate with a geography minor and go from there." Problem number one: There really is nowhere to go from there. Problem number two: The only place hiring graduates with a geography minor was nowhere.

I lived the dream. College was fun. I didn't do terrible my first four years, I just didn't do well enough to fulfill what I woke up every morning for the past 1,400 days to accomplish. The truth was I had no place to go. I'm not saying I couldn't find a job somewhere or go back to get a different degree or specialty, I was simply at the end of this road. I could not go any further in my pursuit. It was an unchangeable situation unless something happened.

I was twenty-one-years-old and living in Mt. Pleasant, Michigan. There are no mountains there. Trust me, I spent years looking. I had no close friends at this point to confide in or ask for wisdom. I was a bit of a wanderer. I wore cardigans and hoodies. So, what does this young man do in this situation? Break. I gave up. I settled in my heart for what was real at the moment, and I stopped running after what I couldn't seem to hold on to. I didn't quit on life or my goals, but I gave up on the "come and see" promises of the world. I let go of what I had chosen to give my life to, which was the pursuit of everything I believed would guide me into a fulfilling outcome. What I didn't know is that by giving up, I would find life. So there I was, on my knees in a small church located in the middle of a field at 11:30 p.m. at night. As I sat there, I pleaded with God to help me. For me, he was all that was left. This was my end. I was exhausted and was done searching. In that moment, it felt as though I had looked everywhere for something that would last. Fortunately in this world, he is always the one thing that will be left. He is the tree that lasts through the winter as the leaves fall.

For six months I began to finish up what was left of my pursuit in college toward a minor in geography, but that was secondary to my pursuit of God. I went after truth full force. I sought after God in the quietness of a local coffee shop, and day after day his Word became my hope. It began to settle in my heart and heal the shame and guilt I had stored up for the past four years of my actions and the way I lived my life. Where I came from as a young boy and knowing of God, had finally taken root in me as a broken young man. What I learned most was that God was unchangeable. I was left (rightly so) by a close friend. The friendships I had were not strong enough to carry through the years and even if they were, they would not have been the answer to what my heart needed most. The pursuit of what kids from Brighton are "supposed to do" was all but lost in a geography degree, but God, he had not left. He was still the faithful presence in my life.

This is the message to all mankind of his love, his care, his presence, and his truth. He will always forever be unchangeable and alive. No matter what may be in front of us, he is unchanging. The grace that he has shown us through the death of his son is sufficient and enough for mankind. It is not powerless against any past or present to save and can change what is changeable—the human heart and mind. But it would take an unchangeable God to change the twenty-two-year-old that I was.

At that time in my life, I began to see that his Word within the Bible was not there to coddle my own desires or interpretation of what I wanted it to say. It was there to convict me in love leading to change, but in that change, I needed to cling to him more and more. So the more God did in my heart, the more I grew in the knowledge of my need for him. The more truth revealed to me, the more I needed him to help me walk in it. This is where I became the changeable one. What I used to come and see for fulfillment or satisfaction, I began to find foolish compared to knowing him through his Word. It made sense that I would be the one in need of a different way of life in understanding what was right and wrong. I could no longer walk in my guilt of trying to justify my actions by ignoring what he was saying, thus saving me from myself. I could no longer look to the proclamations of how the world justified what is right or wrong, what is acceptable, or how life should be lived. Everything had to come under his unchangeable truth to be tested against. Yet, even in this knowledge, I felt the weight and pull of myself to wander back into my old ways and old truths but convicted by his Word to stay with him.

This is where we all find ourselves. We are changeable and influenced so greatly by others. Parents, friends, and people we follow on social media can mold us into who we are today while we follow and watch their lives. All of us have been shaped in some way by the world, but our hearts alone are searched by and held accountable through what is unchangeable truth. This is why humanity longs to be known fully. We want a full life, guided into what is lasting in love and of worth. It's where we will find joy. This life is not found in things accumulated. Life is not found in the places we go, and as hard as it may be to understand this, life is not found in the people around us that we love. These gifts are all from God for our enjoyment, but also for him. All of these examples find their places in time and bring joy to our lives but are under the authority of what God has established as unchanging. Everyone and everything is fading away, and the love we have for them cannot do anything to elongate their lives. No one can truly love someone forever if we die without hope in the end. We may be able to create joy and happiness within this belief for a while, but it will not stop what is the inevitable. We will all break at some point. Our weakness will be revealed. Our need will be revealed. He is the giver of life, beauty, and worth. He alone sustains our lives even through an unavoidable end. He will carry those who trust in him into what lasts beyond what is ever changing, this world. His faithfulness in the darkness will reveal what we need and lead us into truth, which gives life to the full, founded in a hope that is unswerving and never changing amidst the ever-present change of humanity. This is salvation.

As I sought out the Savior, I found my Father. I did get to go back and finish what I went to college to do. I was somewhat confused as to how I got into the education program that my counselor told me I would not get into. Twelve years later I found out my father had made a phone call to the admissions department and spoke with one of the representatives there. I thought it was some crazy coincidence that I was accepted. When I made the error of taking advantage of the freedom I had in college and losing what I so hoped in, my father spoke of what he knew of me. He told the representative of my capabilities and what a great teacher I could be. He spoke with her for a while about his experience as a teacher. He knew who I was while I was still trying to figure that out for myself, just in a different way. By the grace of some people at Central Michigan University, the way was made for me to finish what was left undone by my own fault. This is what it took: my father making a way for me to have what I longed for as he came and spoke on my behalf. It wasn't as if I deserved to get into the education program; I clearly missed that opportunity. But it was the love my father had for me that led him to step into the situation.

Everyone finds themselves at the mercy of God's unchangeable love for the world by sending Christ to this earth for the forgiveness of our sins and wrongdoings. Whether we believe it or not, we are still held accountable to it. And it isn't that we deserved this intervention because we had a great resume or would make a great person to be in heaven with. God intervened in the darkness and hidings because he loved us and wanted us to know him as what he is, our Father.

Amongst mankind, the desires and beliefs we have in today's issues are often based on how they make us feel. They may feel good and right in the moment, but have been tested against what is unchangeable. What is unchangeable will not be influenced by man's thoughts, feelings, entitlement, or ideology of what is good and right. As beautiful as the leaves of our knowledge may seem, they will find an end. They will fall from the tree and reveal their boundaries of life and fullness. Humanity can in no way come before an all-knowing and loving God and change what is in his Word for any reason, even the reason of the pursuit of happiness. I was very happy for the first four years of college. I had a lot of fun, but in the end I needed to break because I saw the leaves fall and the branch left empty. I believed going against what he speaks or changing it to fit my desires and perceived needs would be beneficial and deserved. I did not know that when we try to change what is unchangeable, it no longer leads to life, but an end.

We can be thankful for a God that will never leave us in his love. It is not like the love of a boyfriend or girlfriend, and in the saddest of circumstances, a husband or wife. Millions of people have been left alone and empty in these relationships. His reliability and faithfulness is assured for those who know and trust him. You may have been let down by someone who claimed to love you or have felt abandoned in a relationship, but this is not the love of God. He will not fail even when we fail. His love will not leave us if we did not live up to his standards. He will not point the finger of condemnation as he calls out to the soul of men and women but will turn our gaze to the cross where his Son died, that we may see his love; a love that sacrifices to bring us close to him. He has everything he needs being God, yet gave everything he had to show this world his everlasting, never leaving love. This is our lasting desire if we would only see it, but so often our hearts long for anything that will draw us to the "come and see" of promises that will temporarily meet a deep longing to be loved, known, or accepted. Some of these promises have led to the beauty of life and some to the brokenness. But there will only be one desire that is eternally fulfilled, the desire that God has to save.

Within the changing of what is unchangeable we may celebrate in the fading of our momentary happiness but miss the everlasting joy of knowing the Father that gives eternal life. He leads us to peace. This is where we find rest from trying so hard to prove our worth by posting updates on our social media outlets or passing laws to benefit our desires that may be contradictory to what is right in his unchanging truth. Here we find peace of mind and heart, without shame or guilt, that trumps any momentary pleasure this world or any person could ever offer another. We have found an unchangeable worth in the unchangeable God through his grace, shown and given to us in his Son's death.

He is the unchangeable one. The Creator gets to set the world in motion, sustain it through his provisions and gifts, and establish what is right. Not in the eyes of we who are changeable but in his own eyes. And given time may we break in trying to change his truth within our lives. In our selfishness, may we "come and see" we are the ones in need of change. At some moment may we find the way to change through Jesus Christ and his everlasting Word that carries us into eternity, teaching us to remain and stay with an unfailing love that will never let us go. We are the changeable ones, but it will take light to reveal the need for change within our hearts. He will be the one working in us. It will take time for many to understand and come into this light. Fortunately for this world, he is patient and is waiting for those who will, with time, know him. They will become new in him and through his work alone. Then, we will finally taste what it means to be found in the Unchangeable One, where peace is not based on circumstance but on everlasting truth. For the grass withers, the leaves fall, but His word alone endures, unchangeable forever. This is love for a world in darkness, revealing the way through his Son, this beautiful light. May we see that someone we could not touch, someone so far beyond our reach, has reached out to humanity—leaving us in awe.

CHAPTER 6—THE GREATEST

MUHAMMAD ALI COULD VERY WELL BE THE BEST boxer this world will ever see. He boxed in the 1960s, 70s and into the early 80s. He was a very confident man in his abilities and his in-your-face attitude made for great showmanship of his talents. His most famous saying about the way he fought was a comment on his ability to "float like a butterfly and sting like a bee." This spoke of his quickness and power he had in the boxing ring. He is best known for the statement he made about himself proclaiming, "I am the greatest!" He followed that statement with, "I am the greatest thing that ever lived." Did I mention he was really confident? He was never one to admit he was weak while fighting. Always sure of himself, he fought and defended his title as the world champion three times between 1964 and 1979. He truly deserves that label: "The Greatest." That's the short story of Muhammad Ali's boxing career, but there is weakness and imperfection in him by the names of Norton, Spinks, Holmes, Frasier and Berbick. These were boxers of Ali's time that he fought, some more than once. All of these men, on five separate nights, brought down him whom was supposedly "the greatest". Well, maybe not all to the mat, but in unanimous decision they outfought the greatest. They showed that Ali could be beaten and was not capable of perfection and that even "the greatest" had his limits.

In the end, we are all capable of being taken down no matter how great we think we are. I'm sure at some point, this world has found our weakness. The temptation to live out our addictions to alcohol, drugs, lust, hatred, the struggle in forgiveness, bitterness, and sexual immorality have destroyed individuals and families. They have torn apart friendships and have led to many moments of emptiness in the hearts of men and women. Every day, we find ourselves surrounded by people who are going through these situations. We cannot see someone being beaten down unless we become close enough to them where they reveal what is going on. We then become aware of what is unseen. It's in these moments we glimpse what the love and light of Jesus is capable of.

I found myself walking alongside a favorite trail of mine that runs parallel with the Chippewa River in the Mid-Michigan area. It was fall. I can remember the brisk air cutting through my hooded sweatshirt. I was about to enter the trailhead into the woods when I saw a man slumped over a picnic table just beside the river. I wasn't sure, but I assumed he was homeless and sleeping. I felt compelled to give him the money I had on me. As I approached him, he popped his head up; instantly, I knew he was not well. His nose was running, he began coughing, and his face looked worn out and dirty. The sweatshirt he was wearing was tattered and torn, and his fingernails were filled with dirt. As he spoke to me, he slurred his words.

I gave him the change I had in my pocket and he said, "Thank you." I went on my way. As I walked down the path I knew I had missed an opportunity. I couldn't leave the encounter as I had left it; There was unfinished business. I turned around on the trail and walked back toward him, hoping he was there. Sure enough, he was. His head was once again resting on the table. I sat down and he lifted his head up to look at me. His eyes were yellow and watery. I reached out my hand and held it there for a few seconds before he realized I was offering him more than money. He took my hand and shook it. I couldn't help but notice his fingernails again. I asked if he was hungry and he said, "Yes." I asked him if he liked sandwiches. He nodded his head, and I left to buy him a submarine sandwich. When I came back he was fast asleep again, so I woke him up with a gentle clear of my throat. I gave him his sandwich, but he couldn't control his hands from shaking, so I opened the wrapper for him. He began to talk. I began to listen. The spots began to show.

He told me his name was John. He had just gotten out of jail a couple weeks prior to that day. His words slurred as he coughed, trying to gain some sense of what was happening. He continued and revealed much about his past. The relationship he destroyed with his daughter because of decisions he had made seemed to weigh heaviest on his heart. His abuse of alcohol led him to the abuse of his family, leaving him behind bars. He was now back in the bottle and without a place to lay his head at night. He seemingly sobered up right in front of me when he began talking about his past. His words became clearer and his strength came back to his body. I listened for about twenty minutes and then he went silent. He was finished with his story—but the story wasn't finished.

John was just like us. At some point in his life he believed a lie, and that lie had an origin. There is a reason we have been in darkness, whether past or present. We have an enemy that absolutely hates us. He not only attacks our hearts but also destroys lives by leading us into everything but truth. These lies can be subtle but with blatant purpose in deceiving humanity into searching out what cannot fully satisfy the heart. We will do things that destroy hearts and lives around us within these lies. Our desire to fulfill longings can impact us personally as well as many others. John found this out the hard way: behind bars. Now he had turned to yet another lie; believing that alcohol would quench the pain of what he had done. He is not alone.

Take a look at college campuses: The desperation to be noticed and seen, or to fulfill some longing, becomes destructive to the soul of young men and women as they depend on alcohol and drunkenness to provide the way into what they desire. It's heartbreaking. In my case, it wasn't alcohol but the belief someone else could be everything I needed in life. This belief only took me so far. For many people it could be a great desire to gain value by changing what they look like outwardly, and for others it could be taking advantage of another's heart to meet a physical or emotional impulse within their own lives. You see, the outcome of the lies we believe lead us to destruction. This is where shame and guilt thrive in the darkness we have found ourselves in.

The deeds we commit in darkness only push us further into the hiding. It is cyclical and redundant for many. And the one who lives for the darkness and longs to hold people to it is the father of these lies. He deceives friends, loved ones, and family. He deceives the world; we are not alone. There is a present evil just as there is an ever-present light. No one on their own has willed themselves to overcome the temptations to do what is wrong without the light of truth. We all have fallen for this deceit at times, and in doing so, we have taken on sin and its outcome, death. Just as Jesus leads us to truth and life, Satan's enticements rage in our lack of knowledge without light; leading us to sin, destruction, and death. All humanity lives on this earth within the unseen presence of God, the lover of our soul, as well as the enemy, the deceiver of our hearts and minds. We are vulnerable in the night.

Think about this. Who do we hurt most in our lives by the way we live at times? Those we love the most. The darkness we walk in or have gone through will affect the ones closest to us. And the deceiver will kill, steal, and destroy through the tempting of someone into believing lies and false promises such as, "This will make you feel better. This will satisfy you. Go after it." Satan desires to draw us into selfishness, making our decisions solely based on our own wants, not on the outcome it may have on those around us. This leads to gossip, slander, malice, lust, greed, and all kinds of wrong that affects others we care about. Satan will tempt because he hates and his greatest desire is to destroy lives and relationships, all the while blinding us to the truth that light reveals. This is the truth that leads us to acknowledge our need for the help of the Savior.

To be ignorant of this deceiver is exactly where he desires the human mind to be. To deny his existence is to become apathetic to the light, presence, and truth of Jesus. And if we deny the light we are so in need of, then Satan's hate and deceit has been made complete. We are not alone. Whether in the past, present, or future, we have or will be tempted into believing the lies and may fall short once again before a perfect God. But death and darkness have not overcome. Salvation's story has begun and humanity has a hope beyond our imperfection and this story is not finished—not for you, not for me, and not for my friend John.

There we sat, John and I, listening to the river pass us by at the picnic table. The damage of darkness that he has walked into has taken its toll on him. His outer appearance reflected the current state of his heart. Crushed under the guilt of his actions he sat there silent. After hearing his past, I knew there was nothing I could give him that would make him feel better. I was out of money and food. I alleviated the temporary need; all I had left now was truth. I told John that there is grace and forgiveness for what he has done in his life. I told him that God's grace is greater than his wrongdoings. John began to cry and said, " You don't understand the pain I have caused people." I felt his pain, but didn't let up. I continued to tell him that the death of Jesus was why God sent him. His death gave us life again. It gave us hope despite our past. John began to weep. All

I can remember is him saying, "You have no idea what this means for me. You have no idea how blessed I am because of this." The man was now totally sober. He stood up and walked over to me, took my hand to bring me in for a hug. "You have no idea how I needed to hear this," he said as he cried.

Truth matters to the soul of mankind and saves us from the lies of the deceiver. This light is truth. This Jesus is the light the world needs and his truth alone reaches into and calls us out of the darkness. It will not cause perfection within our brokenness as we live here, but it will guide us into truth that changes lives. Men and women everywhere can now step out of the darkness and into the light. It's time to walk out of the dark because a lasting love awaits us. What mankind has searched for is revealed in the Savior, and his desire is for the soul to cry out to him in their time of need.

This is about you and me. When we can admit that we have fallen here, our eyes can open. When we can admit we have been defeated, we can look up and see the Savior pulling us up off the floor of the boxing ring. Many have taken his hand out of guilt, shame, or hopelessness. Many have found him when they could not get up on their own. He has reached out to all in different ways. He's taking us out of the ring and out of the fight. The amazing thing is that he didn't fight back. He laid down his life instead. He could have, if he wanted to, ended the fight in an instance, but he had to lose first so we would never lose him. We walked where evil treads, and in himself, Christ, took the punishment that leads to death. He knew we would not win this fight on our own. We could not train hard enough nor be good enough to defeat what was holding us. No one is great enough. He had to make a way so that we would not feel the sting of death but the joy of a new beginning. The death that awaited us, the Father put on his Son in the form of a cross. He suffered and bled on our behalf, and what seemed to be defeat was actually where the bout turned. Then the fight was won, and we were given the greatest gift because of the greatest love.

"Love wins." That phrase has been hacked by humanity more than once. Hijacked for our own accord and renown. Celebrated by men and women whose hopes rely on what is seen and felt temporarily, not understanding that no one here can love forever without the everlasting God. The love of humanity will run its course as long as life will allow but will find its end without the Savior. The love God showed on the cross has not overcome so that man can get their way once again, leading us to reject God and his truths, but in a way that God becomes the greatest within the lives of the ones who have been saved. That love is no longer first and foremost about our own desires but simply about a love that truly deserves, in all things, to be rejoiced over most. In the end for everyone, there are only three worthy treasures to be found and none can be seen: Faith, hope, and love, but the greatest is love. This love is Jesus.

The love I speak of is much like what we long for and give to those around us. We see glimpses of its selflessness, compassion, and forgiveness every day. We see humanity live in such a way that stirs our hearts to find and live out such love. But once again, we have walked in darkness. What we offer in love to one another is not capable of overcoming wholly the longing for everlasting love within the human soul. Where we meet our end as men and women, God alone can reach to us. He has reached us.

In the depth of our hearts, we hold to faith and hope. These two treasures are soul-satisfying longings. They resound through our culture in times of pain and in times of triumph. We enter into relationships and marriages based on both faith and hope of something lasting in life. We talk with our friends and families about our hopes of what life could be "if only we made more money", "had a bigger house", "had a better job", "if only he (or she) liked me more". These are just some of the longings we desire to come to fruition. We are absolutely designed to thrive in faith and hope. It is a human quality that no other created thing can live in or experience. It is life giving to humankind here on this earth. It's what separates us from all creation. A God that desires both faith and hope for us, in him, made us. His longing is that our faith and hope will not be found in what will eventually fade, but in what will last beyond what is seen within this life. It will not be overcome by defeat or divorce. It will not be overcome by addiction or poverty. It will not be overcome by hate or anger. It will not be overcome by an unfavorable outcome we may have experienced. And it will definitely not be out fought by evil, shame, guilt, and darkness that have so often brought many to their knees. We have lost and have watched loss happen right before our eyes, but we are told to hold to what is unseen. The one that is unseen cannot be physically touched, but is intimately close in faith. He is the one that picks up our head and tells us to hold on to him. The overcoming will happen.

Love is the greatest treasure because it draws us into worth. Someone has given us value by the way they've invested in our lives. The problem is we give worth to things that are of less worth than the heart. We give people a place of worth based on their outer appearance or worldly credentials. We give special attention to others based on what may be seen, not what is unseen. Yes, we deeply love those closest to us because of their investment in our lives or our lives in theirs, but even the worth we find in that love will eventually be overcome by death. This is not to be seen as insensitive, but reality. It is why we often say, "'til death do we part" when we marry. Love becomes limited when its hope is in humanity. So we must ask the question, "Where do we find our worth?" The answer in our lives will be what we love most; but is it everlasting?

The opposite is said for the love of Jesus. His love alone is pure and sees beyond the physical appearance and outlasts the physical presence of a person. There is a women mentioned in the Bible that had been sleeping with many men and found herself in the presence of Jesus at a well. As she drew water from that well, it was not her beauty that drew Jesus to talk with her. He saw her worth beyond her appearance and her impure past. Being God, he knew her actions were wrong but went beyond a slanderous word or a degrading comment about her life. It was not condemnation that he came to offer people. He offered her something that her heart needed because he loved her. He offered her life everlasting. This is the love of

God for the world. What she could not find in the physical relationships with men—security or worth—she found in the words of Christ as he sat with her. He is not ignorant to our ways. He is all-knowing, and within that knowledge he would look at each one of us and tell us to stop quenching our thirst for satisfaction within the brokenness of sin and empty promises from this world. He is the unending drink of water our soul needs to be at rest and peace. He is enough.

This is his love. It cannot be found in anyone but him. Love belongs to him first. Jesus is love. He is pure love; perfect love. His love finds no end and goes beyond the grave. He cares enough to show us our wrongdoings within the sunsets we live in. What men cannot discern in the fading light, he can. He fully knows who we are within the present darkness we may dwell in. When we begin to see our need for light and life, he is there to save us from that which leads us to death apart from love. This love lasts forever but only attained in Jesus, and his love never fails us. God loved this world so much that he made the way to love forever. Not just to love, but to be loved.

He sees how we have been hurt and how we have caused hurt. Yet, as we take refuge in the shadows of the sunsets, he whispers truth as we walk in the lies. He is not done with you. Even now, love is calling out faith and hope in the hearts of many around this world that are coming out of darkness and into his light. He is reaching those in search of hope beyond the circumstances. Jesus is overcoming through the blood he shed on the cross. People are turning to him in their sunsets, no longer hiding in the fear of sin or what others may think of them. His love keeps no record of wrong because of what his Son did for those who believe. He took the shame and guilt of sin with him as he hung on the cross, so that we may be made right before God. This is the sacrifice of true love: to have someone step in when we were defeated and save us.

Faith and hope being found in the love of God is possible in the belief of Jesus as Savior. The beauty of those found in Jesus is how we reach out because he first reached out for us. It is our Father's trait he has handed down to those who love him; we are now compelled by the one within us to love others the way he loves—in truth. Truth saves. God is into saving the world for the promise of what's to come. His love is the greatest because he stepped into what was an inevitable defeat in the punishment of our sin and took the beating on our behalf to overcome death. In overcoming, we can now know his love. We are loved perfectly—finally.

CHAPTER 7—THE RISING

A TALL METAL CABINET STOOD IN MY DAD'S classroom where he taught for 37 years. His room was located near the back of the school. He had one window that looked out to the side yard and road. Anyone that has a window at work knows they can be thankful. There's something about being able to see more than four walls. He taught History and probably gave out about one million Jolly Ranchers for correct answers from students during his career as a teacher. That was none of my concern because I also knew there were full size Snickers and Milky Way bars in those metal cabinets. He was the head of student council and the middle school dances, so all the candy went through him.

One day, a friend of mine reminded me of those candy bars in his cabinet and asked if he could have one. It was the end of the day and my dad was out of his room. I knew I shouldn't, but I found myself more concerned about what my friend would think of me if I didn't attempt to steal a couple pieces of candy for ourselves. I pulled out a chair and opened the cabinet. There they were, hidden on the top shelf, those brown packages with red and blue writing. I could now taste the chocolate as I began to reach my hand into the box to grab a Snickers. I'm pretty sure I saw drool coming from my friend's mouth while he smiled, waiting to taste the goodness of caramel covered in chocolate. Just as I was pulling my hand out to give him the candy bar, my dad walked in the room. I froze midway through the hand-off. My father got that look on his face and told my friend to leave. He obliged to the request, quickly. I searched in my head for excuses to justify my actions. Maybe he was diabetic and needed some sugar. Maybe he hadn't eaten in three days, and it was an act of mercy, or maybe I tell him I didn't know that it was wrong to give someone candy from the metal cabinet. But I knew there was nothing I could say. I just hung my head, got off the chair and waited.

I thought I was going to get an earful, but I can recall my father saying very little. He did say he was disappointed in me and that I knew better. He was right. He poured his life into me, teaching me how to be respectful, caring, kind, and obedient. I have failed at many points in my life, and this was one of those moments. I was disciplined for what I did that day. But what I also know now is that I needed to be disciplined. I was in my father's care as a child, and it was his responsibility in raising me to know what is right and wrong. That day he saw me stealing candy, and I could not plead ignorance. I could not look him in the eye and tell him I did not know, because he led me into being truthful and not deceitful in my life. I have not fulfilled that perfectly, but through his intolerance of my wrongdoings while teaching me what is right, I now live at peace with others to the best of my ability. When I have hurt others, I know it and have conviction in it. This makes me wonder: What if my father didn't care about my actions and kept to himself? How would that have affected me as a child? What if he was distant? What if he was indifferent and tolerant of all my ways?

Tolerance has somehow become the defining picture of how humanity should interact with one another. We have beautifully linked tolerance with what we perceive acceptance to be. This is difficult because within this life, tolerance can be measured in many ways: how we treat our neighbors who vote differently than us, how we treat those who have different beliefs than us, and how we interact with entire communities who have different socioeconomic standards and lives. We are all called, within tolerance, to be at peace amidst our differences. This is right and this is good within life. But understand it in a way in which Jesus saw this. Was he a peacemaker? Yes. Was he a great teacher of love? Yes. Was he kind to those in need, and did he set an example for all humanity to follow? Yes. All of these he succeeded in perfectly. He was the epitome of inclusiveness in the truth he revealed. If this is true, then why did so many people hate him? Why was he known as one the most radical leaders this world has ever seen as to the impact he had and is still creating? And why did he tell the people who would follow him that the world would hate them too? Did he live in such a way that he desired to create hate and unrest amidst people? He knew it would happen, but it wasn't his purpose in coming. It wasn't the man or the life that he lived that so offended many people in his time. It was what he proclaimed to be truth that leads to eternal life. This is where people wish he had kept to the basics of loving and helping people. The world hoped he would slap a tolerance sticker on his donkey's rear and ride off into the distance while John Lennon's "Imagine" played in the background. But he didn't. He told people he is the only way to the Father God, and he told others to continue to do so. He is the beauty of this good news for humanity and desired us enough to speak this truth out of love. This is why he was hated and rejected.

Now if tolerance is to create peace, then I am in. If it is to keep quiet the message of what can save this world eternally, then I am against it. If this is the case of our tolerance—that truth should find its place in silence—then it can be synonymous with apathy and the strongest form of indifference to life that the world will ever know. We are foolish to believe there are multiple truths that at their core contradict each other greatly. This is not logical nor helpful, only harmful to the soul of men and women everywhere. We all can love and care for another as Jesus taught us to do, but he did not end there. He told others to speak of him and live as him, in love, not in ignorant tolerance. The foundation of his life and message for mankind was to turn away from our sin and darkness, believing in him as the needed Savior for the salvation of our soul. That message was for all people. Does this challenge tolerance within our society? This could be where those that believe in him will find the world beginning to call them intolerant. Not because of their offensive intolerance meant to hurt others, as we have seen poorly represent Christ at times, but as a result of their belief in Jesus and love for the world. This is where the world that screams "Tolerate!" will no longer tolerate the one speaking the message. Thank God he did not end his pursuit of us while tolerating us in our darkness and rejection of truth. Thank God he truly loved us to the point of sending his Son to reveal truth and to die on our behalf. This is where love and tolerance will never find unity.

God in no way tolerated my sin and ignorance of him, nor my wrongdoings within my life. He allowed me at moments to struggle through my own desires to push him out and fulfill my own wants that were against his truth. But at no point was he silent about his Son or silent about my life. I wish for all mankind's sake God tolerated us in our darkness and then let us dwell with him forever in eternity, even if we rejected him, didn't care about him or love him. That is not our God who desires love from his creation. He did not tolerate us to the point of letting us die in our ignorance and sin, because love is not synonymous with tolerance. Love is a passionate pursuit to make things right, not in the view of mankind's perception or determination of what's right, but in the Creator's right to pursue the human heart, soul, and mind. Because of this, we may know him, love him, and dwell in his light apart from darkness forever.

As a father of four, it would cause me great anguish to know my children did not long for truth. Would I still love them? Yes, unconditionally until the day I die. But that would not take away the pain of them forsaking the one who made them to know him as an everlasting Father. So I would plead with God to reveal himself to them that they may reach out for him as their Savior, that his light would invade the darkness that has led them to live apart from truth. I would love them no matter where they were at in life, but I know I cannot give them what Jesus Christ can. I long for them to know what lasts. In this love, I am intolerant of indifference. Above all, I long for them and this world to know truth. Yet I know it is nothing I do. He alone can light our way to truth and life to loosen the hold of the dark.

Just as darkness loses its grip with the morning light, the Son had loosened the grip of death and darkness by rising once again from what seemed to hold him, the curse of sin: death. The sin of the world was placed on him who was perfect and he tasted the curse, but in doing so overcame by rising from it. And as the Son rose, the spots were gone, and the darkness lost its hold. The leaves that hid their blemishes in the sunset showed no spots in those who would acknowledge their need for his light and truth. These spots— our sin—were washed away eternally. Now this promise is for all who believe. So eternal forgiveness, healing, and hope within the brokenness became available to humanity, and life truly began for all who would acknowledge the Risen Savior. Life as it was meant to be, forever with our Father God. We were made right and ready to live eternally with a perfect God.

There is an absolute within this life: Death is ours to taste and at some point, we will. But the casting out of the dark by the light of Jesus is our promise of life beyond the grave. The life found in him will overcome death as light overcomes the dark every morning. Just as he rose from what seemed to be an end, so we are promised the same. A triumphant end to what seems to be an inescapable darkness. The hope in which our last breath would not end in a gasp of air or a tragic accident, but that our final moment here would only be the beginning of true life as it was meant to be: Everlasting.

When I was teenager, I used to travel to Florida every year with my family for Spring Break. The Atlantic Ocean has won my heart. I love its beauty and its waves. My brother and I would swim out into the deep and wait for the waves to come and break over us as we tried to body surf them into the shallow where we could stand, only to swim back out to do it all again. The thrill to be carried along by the power of the waves was a remarkable adrenaline rush, and no amount of time would satisfy or quench our happiness when we were in the ocean.

As a teenager, you take danger on headfirst. One day, within these foolish desires, I thought it would be a good idea to tackle what was an abnormally large surf. The waves were huge and I was going to body surf them if it was the last thing I did. I could see a wave I wanted to catch building behind the set of waves carrying me up and down in the ocean's currents. As this wave approached, I knew I was about to get pummeled and crushed. Still, I threw caution into the wind and went for it. Suddenly, I was lost in a churning mass of water that threw me around like a rag doll in a washing machine. I was powerless against the energy of the wave. As it took me deeper into the water, I realized I didn't know what way was up from down, so I panicked and began to swim. Opening my eyes did not help as I found myself in a sea of sand and water. The sting of the salt burned, so I closed my eyes again and kept swimming.

It took me about five seconds to finally realize I was making my way deeper into the water instead of to the surface. Fortunately, I was a strong swimmer and turned around the way I should be headed, but when I went under the water I did not get a good breath to come through without any problems. I vividly remember that feeling you get when you are running out of the breath within your lungs, the feeling like you cannot possibly squeeze out one more second of air to sustain you. I swam as fast as I could. I had buoyancy on my side that helped me to the surface quickly, but I remember coming up and gasping for a breath that my lungs were so desperate for. As my head broke the surface of the water, my friend's dad reached out for me before I got stuck in the riptide. He pulled me in to get my bearings. The air never seemed so important to me as I exhaustingly swam to shore and admitted defeat for the day.

We take in over 20,000 breaths a day and over 670,000,000 in a lifetime, if we are fortunate enough to get what we would call a full life. Each breath carries with it the great importance of life. It delivers everything our bodies need to function and live. Without air, we suffocate; without breath, we perish. The rising of the Son has provided the breath of life that will always exist for eternity. When Jesus was raised from the dead after dying on the cross, the breath he breathed once again would now be forever, never again to be taken from him by the sin of man. What he did was once and for all final. He gave eternal breath and life to those who would come to know him.

As we have swum in an ocean with the tides of sin, shame, or guilt, his hands pull our heads above the waves as we gasp for air and hold to life. No more fighting the currents of sin and brokenness without hope. It's his hope that carries us to the surface over and over again in this life. It's his voice calling us upward to him as he grabs us in our fight against the tides, his beauty in the brokenness for all mankind. This breath we breathe, first and only in him, is the first in what will be life everlasting through believing his truth. He is the breath of life we all need. As he rose from the dead, we rise from what held us under. His intolerance to watch us suffer under the water led him to the cross, to death, and to rise, so we too would rise from death and the grave. This is true: just as the sun will rise in the morning, the Son has risen from the grave making the sacrifice of his death accomplished and trustworthy. He has faithfully risen as we will faithfully rise into life overcoming death, full of breath and life, for all eternity.

Tomorrow morning we will wake up, as every living person will do at some point around this world. We will come out of our sleep and slumber. Whether we live in India or America, we will rise. The majority will not think about the breath we breathe. Yet with each breath our body tires, accomplishing a purpose within this world as we work, love, laugh, play, or struggle through the day. So, what is needed and what we were designed to do is rest for the morning. We are not capable of functioning without this rest every evening. We are guided by light to sleep and to wake up. Rest and awake; the light calls to us. We are asleep in the dark, but awake in the light.

The light of the world has called us from our slumber. We are not made to sleep in the grave. He himself is not within the ground. He is not to be found anywhere within the earth resting in peace. He is actively working through his truth to create peace between God and man. The savior is alive, and he is giving life and breath to those dead in their sin. To those looking for a hope beyond an ever-failing pursuit of the things that have left us wanting, he is there. He is ready for those that will reach out to him. As our heads rise up from the water's edge, he pulls us through. What was dead becomes alive in the Son. In a hope that is set fully on him, we can live. And as our bodies may rest, our soul will never rest in its longing for life with him forever. May you hear his voice speak to your heart and say, "Come alive!" May you hear him tell you once and for all to stop searching in the depths of the waves for what can only be found above its tides. May we all see that we have run in vain only to be overcome, and in those moments, may we hear his voice telling us to wake up and rise. Let our hearts and minds be focused on what is not seen, but on what is to come. True life begins in the hope of what is yet to be seen by the children of God, a place where we will no longer experience brokenness and a place void of the sun. Here, God will be our light forever. It's a place where we will never run weary or tire. This is our hope. Oh, that you will be one to rise to him and find his peace. The breath we take on this earth will soon find its end. With every breath we breathe may our eyes open, not to a crashing wave, but to the one who has promised to fulfill what he has told us he would do in his truth. One day we will rise with him, and what is temporary will be lost in what is eternal.

CHAPTER 8—THE INVITATION OF HOPE

IT WAS 1998, AND IT FINALLY HAPPENED. THIS NOT-so-cool kid got a date to the prom. I had been avoiding this moment for four years. I had been asked to go to dances before, but I could never push the commit button on dressing up and spending the evening with someone dancing to Jewel or Shania Twain in front of others. I did not want to ask anyone in fear of awkward rejection, but my mother said I should give it a shot. So, I processed through all the possibilities of how this could go wrong and the chance for the experience outweighed the fear. I committed.

With all the courage I could muster up I grabbed the phone and headed for my room. I remember stumbling over my words as I finally got to the point of asking one of my friends to the dance. She accepted. I hung up the phone and thought to myself, "What did I just do?" I had no idea how to pull off what I just walked into. Until this point, I had no experience going on a date with someone.

On the night of the prom, my mom let me borrow her Pontiac Grand Am. Yes, that was the nicest car we could find. I picked up my date on the way to meet up with another couple. I felt very uncomfortable in my tux. I didn't like dressing up, but it was necessary for the occasion, so I went with it. I saw my date and immediately knew I was out of my league. It was unnatural for me to wear such nice clothes at this stage in my life, and I felt like I was fighting my tux, as if someone was trying to choke me. My date, on the other hand, seemed to have no problem dressing up because she looked like she was auditioning for the Miss America pageant. As she walked out of her house with her gown flowing and professional hairdo, I knew the Grand Am was not going to be enough to level the playing field on this night. It was going to be okay, though.

Things started off decent. I took pictures with my friend, his girlfriend, and my date for the evening. We went out to dinner at a nice restaurant and headed for the dance. Everyone looked so different. I was used to seeing my friends wearing jeans with Pearl Jam or Nirvana T-Shirts. In suits, they looked weird to me. As the dance went on, I did my best to get over my fear of actually being at prom by throwing down some sick dance moves. My performance was below par for sure. It was all going well up to this point, but I had a sneaky suspicion this wasn't going to end as pretty as it started.

About halfway through the dance, my date started getting "sweet" with another guy, dancing with him...a lot. As the introverted boy I was, I found a corner and sat with my friend Mason. I was fortunate he was a lot like me and not a natural dancer. Time passed and my date danced with this guy more and more. A week after the dance they began dating. Thanks Mom! How's that for giving it a shot? I gave it a valiant effort to do this thing called prom, but it just wasn't meant to be.

Proms and high school dances, weddings, bridal and baby showers, as well as birthday parties, are a part of our culture. Anytime someone is offered to go on a date there is a silent statement of, "I would like to get to know you more." Yet even in this, there is an unknown outcome of how things turn out. In most of these examples, actually getting invited to these events makes the statement, "I value you." But if we never receive or acknowledge the invite, we may never know what comes with it. It's the invite that tells someone they are of worth in the eyes of the one taking the first step in the invitation. I am glad I had the experience of going to prom. It made for a story, and I overcame a fear. The most difficult part of the whole event was making the initial phone call, because without me taking that step it would have never happened.

This is at the heart of the reason for Jesus: him taking that first step that would eventually lead to the invitation into hope. His death and resurrection spoke to the world of the worth and value we have in God's eyes. The message of what he has done for humanity is good news for all. It is absolutely beautiful. It is news that tells us what needed to be done was accomplished. There is no need to get all dolled up or put on your best vest. There is no need to compete for a crown at this event. There is already a King. He has always been King, but he lived mostly to serve and love others, ultimately to his death. The good news of his coming, his death, and his rising is the invitation for mankind to have life and life to its fullest. This fullest is forever. It is not held by death. It is lived out in love and for what is lasting. As we live in him, we live in an eternal hope assured of the outcome.

Eternal hope is everything within this world and the true definition of what beauty could ever be defined as. No one can deny the desire to love and be loved. This is where what is unseen will never disappoint. It's founded in faith alone and revealed in truth. It speaks to the deepest parts of our heart and soul of the joy in what's to come and makes the fear of the unknown, the worries of life and hardships we will walk in, an opportunity to hold much tighter to the hope of what will never fade, his promises to his children.

I met my future mother-in-law in 2002, a couple years before I married her daughter. She was about 5'2, small in stature, but a giant when it came to love. Her passion in life was helping mothers learn how to take care of their babies. She showed these women what their children will need and how to accomplish basic tasks to meet those needs. She was kind, hospitable, and a lot of fun to be around. Many of us have mothers that make it easy to laugh with and at them. This was my mother-in-law.

Her name was Maureen. Her story is one written with great joys weaved with seemingly hopeless situations and hard times as many of us can relate with. Her brother Kevin was killed in a motorcycle accident, and her younger sister lost a battle to cancer at a young age, leaving behind a sweet little girl. Once again, no one can avoid brokenness of what is seen within our lives. The things we can visually see happening to family members or watch others go through is difficult. This is why we can never fully hope in the seen things of life but only in what is unseen. We never fully know what tomorrow will bring for any of us.

For anyone that has walked with someone while they were dying, you know it is heavy. It demands great emotional strength and perseverance. At times the strength seems sufficient, and at other moments it seems an impossible task to accomplish. My family had to go through this with my mother-in-law. It was heartbreaking as we watched our father take her to appointments and treatments, driving her to cities hundreds of miles away while seeing her unable to live and love as she so desired. She did her best. Her husband was valiant and determined in fulfilling his vows he had made, 38 years prior, to love her in sickness and in health. Then, the moment we all were afraid of happened.

She was done fighting. She looked at her children and her husband from her hospital bed and said, "I'll only be there a couple minutes before you." She was not talking about a different location or some other hospital room. She was speaking of what is eternal and unseen because she fully believed what is unseen is eternal. My mother-in-law knew the everlasting God. She belonged to him. She was his daughter. Even in her care and love for others, she acknowledged her need for his grace. On her knees in prayer, she grew with him throughout her life. She did not pray out of obligation or the need to fulfill some requirement of religion. She genuinely loved God as a Father. She hoped greatly and asked boldly for hope and salvation for family and people along her path. At this moment, she knew her time was coming to an end in this world. She believed what was seen was only momentary, and in that knowledge, she was ready to finish the race that began when she breathed her first breath as a baby. That little girl who grew up to be a wife, mother, friend, and light to so many had reached the finish line of her race, sure of the hope she lived in while here on earth. There was no question whether Jesus would come through on his promises that she held onto. He would.

"I'll only be there a couple minutes before you." Lasting hope cannot be measured in time. The best my mother could come up with at the moment was this: no matter how many years it was until those standing around her bed would pass from this life, it would only feel like a couple minutes to her. The hope she was measured in through Jesus was eternal, never ending and never failing. This is where hope overcomes any obstacle or circumstance the human heart will have to tread through within this life. It will not make everything easier, but it will be the anchor of the soul that will hold us firmly to truth, reminding us of the overcoming of darkness that the light of the world accomplished. Even as we walk in the shadows of the valley in hard times, we see a light shining through to illuminate the hope of what is unseen. He will eternally come through for those who hold tight to his truth and take hold to the invitation of hope.

This invitation will come when you hear about Jesus truthfully. Not by what we may want to hear of him but of truly who he was and what he actually taught in his Word. It will reveal his love, and it will cut to the heart to convict. It will also encourage and heal. All these ways are done for one reason: that you may become a child of God. That's the invitation the human heart has longed for: to be loved, known, understood, never abandoned, and rescued by a Savior from what is fading to what is lasting. Unlike other invites you may receive in life, this one will not suggest you look a certain way or bring a gift as you come.

The invitation to know the Savior simply says "Come As You Are". This is not a moment to purchase a new dress to look better on the outside so others may think of you as "having it all together." This is not a moment to wait until you have done some good things to feel more worthy to respond to the invitation. God literally means come as you are. His heart is for the outcast, the forgotten, the left behind ones abandoned in this world. The mistreated, the sorrowful and seemingly hopeless are the apple of his eye. His words are spoken to the rich, the poor, the prostitute, the addict, the young and the old. His words go out to a world that has hidden in sunsets to temper the feeling of shame or emptiness. His love is for the sinners of this world. There may have been other ways to impress as you responded to different invitations in life, but this invite goes beyond what you look like or how you feel at the moment. Simply come as you are.

You may feel like you have really been doing well and good enough to receive this invite, but you know in the deepest recesses of you heart that you still are in need. You may feel so lost in a mess that you got yourself into. You may have believed that someone or something would satisfy you fully and give you everything you needed, but the heart is left untapped without his presence. You may simply be broken, nowhere left to go, and in need of someone to say, "I'm here, I am listening, and I can help." You may be one that has heard his name or has been down that road before but have recently gone your own way. Maybe you feel now is the time to turn around. He will not reject the one who turns to him. One thing is for sure: We all will have to turn at some point within this invitation, and that turning will mean change. But the turning will be from what leads to death as we walk into his life and light. This invitation is for everyone to walk out of darkness of sin or guilt, brokenness or hurt and into his truth. It's "come as you are", and the gift waiting when you acknowledge your need for him and receive the invitation is called grace. That's why we simply just come. No matter how sinful we may feel, grace abounds. No matter how much wrong you have done, his grace is more. It is sufficient. The forgiveness of God is a wave of righteousness overwhelming the condemnation of our sin. He did not come to condemn, but to save. The forgiveness found in Jesus is enough to cover your shame in love and make what was unattainable—a relationship with God himself—the joy of our hearts as light overcomes the darkness.

For many people, when and if they hear his voice, they will respond and finally break. This could lead you into a desire to know more about him. You should do whatever you need to do to meet that desire. Some may simply want to hear more about the message of this Jesus. Some may hear without truly hearing, as if this was just another good thought but not worth their time. Even so, the invitation stands. It is not offered for only a day, week or yearlong event, because God is not done saving yet. No matter how one would respond to this invitation, the belief in Jesus will continue to save this world. At some point may he call to your heart as you begin to understand what comes with acknowledging the need for him. The promise is not that your life will be perfect. In fact, it will remain difficult at times within the brokenness that is evident on earth. But Jesus will always be there through the end and into eternity, saving those who have trusted in him, while giving them the right to be called children of God. This right alone is found in the saving name of Jesus. This invitation is for all who would hear and believe in him as they acknowledge their need, a Savior. The entire world has been invited into hope, and it must be heard so that those he calls out to may know they can simply come as they are.

CHAPTER 9—THE END

BRIGHTON, MICHIGAN, IS AND ALWAYS WILL BE home for me. I may never live there again, but it is where I knew simplicity and trust. It is where, in the recesses of my mind, I will always find joy and peace. There is only so much I can say to describe the feelings of my youth and where I grew up. It is a special place to me. There was a sense of peace that existed in childhood that is hard to find as one gets older. Yes, peace is still there, but with age comes worry. Trust is the antidote to worry. My antidote as a child was my father.

I can recall my father taking my brother and I to the football games at the high school and walking to the Mill Pond to feed the ducks popcorn. The parades that went though town were moments when the community could experience life as it is meant to be: with friends and family, celebrating whatever the occasion would be. People gathered for a moment to separate their lives from what might be troubling them to know rest and peace, even if it was only for a brief time. My father was always there. As a young boy I did not often worry, because I trusted my dad.

I was at peace and had joy because I knew my father was for me and that he enjoyed being with me. That was enough for my heart.

This is what it means to be a child. This is where life flourishes. It's not found in making more money or impressing co-workers and old friends with our large houses, cool cars, or accolades. It's not by building ourselves up with our words about all we have accomplished, hoping others flock to our greatness. It is found in joy. Life is measured in joy and peace. My heart breaks that we have lost this sense within our society. We see the troubles of life overcoming the young and old, sometimes to the point of death. We see marriages break because of selfishness. We see pain throughout the world caused by man's greed and lust for more. What God has given us, we have claimed in our sin and have used it for our own desires, which now sows itself in the brokenness of where we live. What was so natural about being a child was traded in at some point, and we began to worry more as we listened to the world tell us the path of gain. In doing so, we lost the joy of innocence before our Father. What was home—a place of peace and consistency—has become inconsistent in many lives. It has left us exhausted while we try to figure out life in the sunset, this false beauty where we can hide the truth of our heart's real condition. We live longing for this place of peace where all can be known and loved perfectly.

To become a child once again, not in a physical form but in a spiritual transformation, is joy for the human heart. This is our ultimate purpose: to forever be children of the Heavenly Father. We are reminded through his Word that in his Son, Jesus, we are just that. We now have the father we have longed for. His love is perfect without any fault, failure or broken promise. This is how children walk through life, relying on the faithfulness of their father. We come home even when we've wronged him, and he speaks truth to us while teaching us his way of what is right. He renews the way we think and view the things of this world. He helps us discern what is right and corrects us when we are in the wrong. He teaches us how to have true peace while guiding us into truth. He is incapable of leading without love in the way he cares for us. Whether we need discipline or encouragement, he does so in love. He calls us into light and reveals the freedom from the darkness found only in him. He points to his Son as our example and never leaves us, even in our darkest hour of life. In pain, hurt or sin, he never leaves us. Yet he calls out to us as a father would do, desiring us to look to him for the help we may need. This would not be attainable without the work of his only Son: his life, his death and his rising. There would be no way to come home, no way to find home. We would be lost in the darkness of the night calling for help.

So what does the loving Father, Creator of heaven and earth, do with those who turned and tried to live apart from him? He makes the way home. It's not a GPS guide to follow, hoping you make all the right turns along the way to arrive at the correct place. It's not gained through perfection of following directions. It is not found anywhere that satellites can lead you, and it's not found where the promises of this world can take you. You were meant to dwell and live with God. We could not experience this because of our rejection of him and disobedience through sin. Remember, God cannot have fellowship or a relationship with darkness. In his pure light, only pure light can dwell. So the way was made for those that were living in the darkness to live in his light. Jesus Christ is the light. He loves us so deeply that sinners may be sinless before him through the death and resurrection of his Son. The sin and brokenness we have experienced in this life will not hinder us from going home someday. His work is not finished in any of our lives. He is calling us to stop hiding from him and to be known by him in his light. As a father calls out for his kids in the distance, he has called to us in our sin.

My father used to call out to my brother and I through a very loud distinct whistle. We could be two miles away and still know if it was him by the way the sound would ring through the air. The pitch would go from high, to low, to high. My brother and I would always respond with, "I'm coming!" This was usually a subtle reminder that dinner was on the table. What better way to get two young boys home than telling us food was waiting.

We knew who was calling out to us. We knew what our father had for us was good. He was not calling out to condemn us or hurt us. He was not waiting for us at the door only to tell us he is leaving us. He was not calling out to us only to hide form us as we searched for him. We knew he was trustworthy, and in return, we trusted him. Trust—it is life to our souls and our hearts. Fathers are not supposed to leave, ever. We see the damage this has done to friends, family and loved ones who have gone through those experiences. When a child lacks trust in a father, the relationship is hindered—it is not right. Many times that child decides to hand their heart to something or someone else. This world provides many options when that happens. We have all been vulnerable with our trust. We have handed our hearts over to wolves at times, and we were devoured by deceit. God has done us no harm to discount him from our trust. This world has broken us because it is broken. We are all vulnerable to heartache and pain because of it. It is not God's fault. We marry thinking we have reached the pinnacle of perfection only to realize we married someone that has been broken and struggles with trusting fully at times. That's the beauty of life and humanity: We all play on the same field of trust. We all long for trust that will never fail. Our hearts cry out for a love that will never leave us alone, even in the hardest moments: A love that will make things right again. A love that will bring peace to the chaos, and a love that will make good on its promise. This love that will carry you through and bring you home, the place where you can, once again, live in peace established through trust.

Do you hear God today? Can you hear him calling out to you? Do you find yourself content in the sunset, hiding amidst a world that will never fully know the depth of your heart? There is only one left to trust fully. There is only one left to give your heart to fully. He made you, and he knows you. He loved you enough to give himself so you could be at peace with the Father who desires to save us. Where does your trust lie? Are any of us really capable of living like we can impress God on our own goodness and standards? Do we see that what we could not do, he had to do for us? He made it possible to overcome this temporary, fading world and truly live at home with him.

This all depends on whom you give your heart, soul and mind. My hope is that you will trust the message of his Word. That God so loved you that he gave his Son, Jesus, over to death for you. There's hope that someday, at some moment, you may just reach out to him, believing that he loves and can save you to a true hope. That your heart would be overwhelmed by his mercy and grace for your life, no matter the depth of shame or guilt you may feel. That the brokenness this world has poured out into your heart may begin to heal, so that you too may live this life finding great purpose in continuing the message of hope to others: this message that leads us home, and this message that tells of the Father calling us his children forever.

Do you hear his voice? My deepest hope is that he reveals something to you that you need to hear. I don't know what that is, but I believe he desires you and he just may speak to you. You have heard this many times in the past or maybe you haven't, but I want to say it again. Jesus loves you. He is real. He is not just a historical figure. He is not dead. He is God. He is for you to know him. You are meant to live forever with Him. You are more than a momentary creation, and you need a Savior. You have great worth in the eyes of your Creator. There is no love in this world that you will find that will be everlasting. Alone, he is unfailing. You can trust his words and his love. He will not fail you, even in the end.

We experience endings so many times in this life. Endings typically lead to another experience that will yield another end. Middle school to high school, high school to college, and college to what we hope is a job, are end points some go through. Within these times we find that friendships of the past can sadly come to an end, marriages can come to a close, and the security of a job can be lost. Many moments we hoped would last forever find their limits in time. The beauty of these endings is they often lead us to new beginnings. The same is said for hoping in this Savior. We are not ignorant of an end, but are we trusting in the unending God? There is no beginning or end to his existence. He has always been himself. His promises find no end to those who hold to him. Even in a world that will continue to reveal it's endings, the promises of the unending God will forever be new, not growing old nor coming to a close. This is the world's everlasting hope: that he will be the beginning of who will always be our Father.

Nowadays I find myself looking out the window of my house at that same maple tree we began this book with. The tree's spots are not noticeable from where I sit, but they are there. Out the back window of our kitchen my kids play in the yard in the fading light of the evening. The sun begins to hide itself in the trees as it makes its way out of sight. Life happens here in sunsets. We all have gone through and live with them. Even in these sunsets, we still see the beauty of humanity and what God has created. We still sense the worth of what God has made even if it is broken. I have lived in sunsets. I have hidden in the night. I still struggle against the temptation to find rest there. I know what it feels like to withhold my heart from others because I haven't trusted at times. But then light comes and shines on me, revealing this heart and turning my eyes to my helper. Where I tried to hide from Jesus, his love called out to me. He saw me in my shadows and in my sunsets when no one else could. He saw my beauty despite the darkness. He knew what was wrong and took every sin. Jesus took the spots and blemishes of my life upon himself and saved me. No longer can I hide in the darkness, I am called into his light. I am fully seen and fully known. His light is in those who are saved. I am not perfect. I still do wrong against my Father, and in those moments, I am aware of his grace. But in his unchanging love and promise, I still walk in his light. He will never leave me. Do you believe this for yourself? Is this your hope? Is light your longing or is darkness your comfort? Is the sunset your home and hiding place, or is his grace where you rest your heart?

I can still remember hearing the train making its way to the intersection as I listened from my bedroom as a child. I can almost feel the depth of the sound coming from its horn. The distant sound of the tracks carry along the cars, becoming louder as the train gets closer. I sit there in silence, watching the light of the sky making its way around the world as it begins to fade for the evening. This light is shining on all mankind, revealing its faithfulness to everyone who will wake the next morning. For a moment we will sleep, but the day will bring a new joy for the child that longs for the light. That 7-year-old boy still longs to be known as a child, even as a 36-year-old man. There is a desire to be found in an unfailing hope and trust as faithful as the sun. And as I write these words I can remember that back window of my childhood home like it was yesterday.

It's where peace was at its greatest as the sun began to set. I knew the sun would come back in the morning. I knew the night would end. I knew I would be able to live as a child another day. My heart looked forward to a new morning as I watched the sunset and listened to the train.

As life passes, that longing is still there. Someday, when the end does come to my time, as it will come to all, I will be a child. I wait for peace to be known at its fullest within this hope where all struggles and troubles will never meet this heart again. For some, it's a constant worry. For some, it's an exhaustion brought on by hurt or the pursuit to have or look more like your neighbors and friends. For others, it's loss. The loss of trust or the loss of someone you loved deeply. It could be the loss of what someone held so tightly to or put their hope in. These struggles will be overcome in the presence of peace and light and the joy they bring. The joys of this life are just a glimpse of life with God. The laughter and love we have are just a taste of what's to come for those found in Jesus. Heaven is a childhood home the soul desires most in those that are being saved.

I love this life. I am thankful for each breath and the time I get to live here with family and friends. We continue to experience life as long as breath is present, yet you and I have no guarantees for the next breath. So I will tell you with confidence, this is not my home. It's simply the window I wait and watch from. I can see the hurt of the world and know it for myself because I am living in and around the sunsets momentarily. But this darkness cannot overwhelm the hope I have in the light. For now, I may know brokenness, I may know sin, but I am longing to glimpse the face of the one that brought me to my Father by taking my sin with him to the cross and rising from the grave. Despite those things I hid from others, I could not hide from him. He found me in the darkness and revealed what I needed: a Savior. And where my Father is, is where my home will forever be—no more sunsets, no more darkness, and no more sin.

Here there is only joy and peace, a place where brokenness has no hold. Where no one will hurt nor be hurt, and where we were made to dwell and live. This world is not meant to last, and this world will not last. Our help has arrived. We were in need of help and the Savior has lived up to his name. This beauty, love, and acceptance we've so longed for has found us in the present darkness. In our helplessness, he has heard our cry.

And if today you hear God's voice, I hope you would respond in knowing that he cares about you. In that response, may you find hope in the darkness. May you heal if you are broken. May you know that God loves you deeply. May you become a child before the everlasting Father. And then, in the end, may you find yourself home— fully known, fully loved, forgiven and spotless— at peace with God, in the light of day.